ROMANCE-411

A Tactical Guide for the Romantically Challenged

Sgt. Traci

What Others Are Saying:

"Traci is a romantic genius. Her ideas are fun, clever and fresh. I plan on using several of them myself."

Michael Webb
Best Selling Author
Founder of TheRomantic.com

"Romance-411 is a touchdown!"

"The Grave Digger"
-Gilbert Brown #93
Green Bay Packers
Super Bowl 31 Champions

"Sgt. Traci's book provides realistic strategies and practical tactics for improving your love life. So listen up recruits!"

~ Greg Godek
Best Selling Author
"1001 Ways to Be Romantic"

"Traci, Your Mission: Teach Only Love!"

Dr. Wayne Dyer,
Best Selling Author

"OPERATION ROMANCE Scores the Winning Point!"

Gerry Ellis #31
Green Bay Packers

"Traci takes an unconventional, guerrilla approach to romance and love. If you want an unforgettable experience, try the "Bogan Island" dinner. It's not the same old romantic kitsch and you'll find that romance flows easily, just the way it's supposed to."

-Mark S.A. Smith
Co-author Guerrilla Negotiating

"Traci Keeps Romance on the Move!"

"The Golden Boy"
-Paul Hornung
#5 Green Bay Packers
HOF 1986

"I have always been a believer in developing relationships one MOMENT at a time. Romance-411 is the perfect guide to developing MOMENTS for your partner AND yourself. If you love your partner - you must own this guide to the CELEBRATION of each other."

-Barry Spilchuk
Co-author - A Cup of Chicken Soup for the Soul™
Founder - You're My Hero™ Books

"For all of you entrepreneurs out there who spend all of your time working and hear from your significant others how jealous they are of your laptop! This book will give you some great ideas about how to spark your NON-BUSINESS relationship.

Remember- WELL-ROUNDED = HAPPY!"

-Kelly Perdew
Winner of the 'The Apprentice'
Managing Director,
Angel-Led Venture Partners

"We all want more romance and this book will help stimulate yours. Enjoy!"

-Mark Victor Hansen
Co-creator, #1 N.Y. T. best selling series Chicken Soup for the Soul ®
Co-author, Cracking the Millionaire Code and The One Minute Millionaire

"A lovely lady! A 'Super Bowl' of a book!"

-Fuzzy Thurston
#63 Green Bay Packers

"Our thanks to Sgt. Traci. Her works offer us, not only, a charming recipe for relishing romance ...but also the opportune ingredients for attaining joy and happiness; the result of loving."

-Sandy Sullivan
Author, Green Bay Love Stories
Public Speaker and Educator
2006 Candidate, WI Secretary of State

"Romance-411 is "packed" with idea's that will make you a champion of romance."

Bob Jeter
Green Bay Packers
Super Bowl I & II Champions

SATORI PUBLISHING
Publication Date: 2007

10 9 8 7 6 5 4 3 2 1
ISBN #978-0-9795069-0-1
ISBN #0-9795069-0-5

Edited by Valerie Hennen and Marielle Marne of A-1 Editing
Cover Design Concept by Traci R. Bogan
Graphics Design by Donovan Scherer
Typography by Stratton Graphic Design, Kenosha, WI

Romance-411: A Tactical Guide for the Romantically Challenged is the first product of OPERATION ROMANCE™, LLC. Denoting a series of products and services including books, calendars, invitations and coupons, product kits, gift collections, CDs and DVDs, seminars, workshops, boot camps, and TV. OPERATION ROMANCE™ became incorporated in 2005, by its founder, Traci R. Bogan and is a registered trademark. Please visit our Website: www.OperationRomance.com

OPERATION ROMANCE™, LLC has four divisions:
- Sgt. Traci's Boot Camps™ (Seminars, workshops, & speaking)
- Romance Gram™ (Product kits & gift collections)
- University of Romance™ (Books, calendars, CD's, DVD's and TV)
- Charity: OPERATION EDUCATION™ &
  OPERATION CONSERVATION™

Author contact:
OPERATION ROMANCE, LLC.
P.O.Box 085896
Racine, WI. 53408-5896
1-877-4-SGT-TRACI
SgtTraci@OperationRomance.com
www.OperationRomance.com

While the author has extensively researched all of her sources to ensure that the information contained in this book, at the time of its publication, is accurate and complete, please be advised that business names, locations, Websites, e-mail addresses, and phone numbers may change and/or the companies may go out of business. Neither the author nor the publisher accepts any responsibility for errors, inaccuracies, omissions, or other inconsistencies contained here-in, including but not limited to any slights or unintentionally offensive material. The author is happy to receive corrections, comments, and suggestions for future editions.

This book is intended to be used a reference guide. The material in this book is intended for consenting adults only. The reader assumes 100% of the responsibility for his or her actions and reactions regarding all scenarios, suggestions, ideas, and recipes contained within this book. Execute them at your own risk! The author, publisher, and chef will not be held liable for or responsible to any person or entity with respect to any mishaps or damages caused, or alleged to be caused, directly or indirectly, by any information contained within this book. The author, publisher, and chef do not personally endorse any content therein of the Website addresses referenced in this book. The Web addresses listed are not necessarily personal recommendations; they are simply offered as a reference point that may offer services of interest and/or products to suit perspective needs.

This book was written based on the perspectives, experiences, and opinions of the author. It does not imply that she has personally tried every idea, reference, or suggestion stated within. Please note that while the romantic scenarios are based on actual events, some of the names have been changed and some of the stories have been edited or enhanced by the author to make for a more stimulating read.

N. C.

Thank you for warming my soul with yours
...even if only for a moment, in this 80 year dream.

This book is dedicated to my other loves:

Dr. Wayne Dyer
For leading me to the path and enlightening me with your glow.

To my sister, Jennifer
For sharing with me the two greatest gifts of all,
my handsome Prince, Andrew and my pretty little lady, Tayler.

Amy Shay
The best friend I ever had. With gratitude for changing the course of my life.

Table of Contents

About the Author

Born in Racine, Wisconsin, Traci has always worked to improve the lives of those around her. In 1992, she spearheaded a campaign dubbed "The Bogan Bill" to enact legislation that increased the criminal Statute of Limitations for sex crimes against children. It was largely due to her persistent efforts and grassroots lobbying that the law was changed in 1994.

Never interested in being idle, Traci created her next challenge by moving to Hawaii (with $800.00 in her pocket) where she continued working in the medical field. Traci completed several additional training programs and earned the necessary certifications to work in a variety of medical practices, beginning in the Emergency Room and ending in the Operating Room. Her favorite job up until this point in her career was working for world-renowned plastic surgeon, Robert Flowers. After a decade of work in the medical field, Traci decided it was time to trade her stethoscope in for a compass and fulfill her lifelong dream of seeing the world.

Her travels began crisscrossing America, but soon she broke free of her continental boundaries and completed a twenty-three country world tour. She traversed the physical peaks and valleys of the land, all while experiencing the spiritual peaks and valleys that come with self-discovery. For many lonely nights on strange beds in unfamiliar lands, she had only her own thoughts to wrap around herself each night, and she dreamed of love. As she traveled she asked people she met about love in their lives and she marveled at the common bond that love created between complete strangers. After spending four months in India, she was renamed "Carry Prema" by Vinod Kumar, a yoga guru. Kumar felt the moniker, meaning "Wherever you go, bring love," personified her desire for improving her own life and her passion for helping others to be better in their relationships. After her abrupt return to America (due to illness), Traci discovered that she had a message and a calling to share the importance of love and romance with the world; This first book and her company, OPERATION ROMANCE™, is an attempt to fulfill that prophecy. A romantic at heart, she shares these highlights as well as many of her own well received ideas.

From a whisper in the wind great storms grow; and so has Traci's message. Traci experienced an epiphany in her life when she realized that the secret to a happy and healthy relationship is to have a happy and healthy self. Traci knew she had to bring her concept of "US Begins With U" to a world filled with broken marriages, unhappy couples and lonely people; but in order to change such a fundamental philosophy it would take more than one woman, it would take an army.

Traci began to teach her concepts to individuals she recruited into Operation Romance Boot Camp and soon took on the persona of Sergeant Traci the no-fluff pseudo drill Sergeant who teaches individuals (recruits) about true intimacy, vulnerability, letting go of past battle scars, and the romance secrets she learned from the other side of the world and from her own heart. (See end pages for Boot Camp details.)

Traci recently earned a degree in Marketing (with President's honors). As Sgt. Traci, she is touring the United States conducting her seminar Boot Camps and growing the ranks of Operation Romance™.

Acknowledgements

After many title changes, cover theme adjustments, and detailed edits, ROMANCE – 411 is finally finished and has become all I hoped it would be! I am eternally grateful for everyone who believed in me and to everyone who didn't; you each gave me the exact motivation and determination that I needed to make my dream a reality.

Shortly after the return from my world tour, I decided to follow my dream and pursue a new career as an author, trainer, and entrepreneur. I enrolled at Gateway Technical College to pick up a degree in Marketing and take some business and finance classes. It didn't take long for me to discover the unlimited resources that were available to me at Gateway, and soon my quest for a published book became more like a "school project." Students, teachers, and advisors alike all banded together to help make my dream a reality. We held contests from romantic cuisine recipes to marketing plans and book cover designs. Hundreds and hundreds of hours of help came from all corners of Gateway, from editing and formatting to layout and web design. I was even assigned five of my own personal interns! (Brian Barnes, Brea Quadracci, Susan Walter, Donovan Scherer and Tracy Drake.) Gateway Technical College has been instrumental in the timeliness of my book's release and in the planning and progress of my forthcoming business, OPERATION ROMANCE™. A heartfelt thank you to the teachers and advisors who lent their time and expertise and offered me their friendship: Valerie Hennen, Cheryl Ucakar, Ray Koukari, Jr., John Mizer, Sue Hanneman, Joan Paradiso, John Gauthier, and Faye Mueller. A special thanks to each of my fellow Marketing classmates who band together and lent themselves to my dream, using it as a theme for numerous class projects. Further appreciation goes to WMMA (Wisconsin Marketing Management Association) and Dex (Delta Epsilon Chi) for creating the platform on which futures, dreams, and entrepreneurs are built. I am thrilled and privileged to be a part of this association and can't wait to give back as an alumna!

The final version of this book would not have been possible without my right-hand woman, Lael Grigg, whose suggestions, input, and energy led her to wear the hat of a friend, brainstormer, consultant, editor, graphic designer, photographer, and researcher, just to name a few. Special thanks to Chef Tory Miller for his brilliant artistry and for sharing his delicious recipes with me, to Traci Miller for her creative suggestions and her desire to share the restaurant's proceeds with the L'Etoile Farmer Fund. And especially for sharing her Office Manager, Lael Grigg to see this project through to completion. And to my personal friends and mentors, Greg Godek, Victor Gonzalez and Dale Froehlich for running the distance with me.

And last but certainly not least, to my friends and contributors of "the first draft" that seems so long ago, who stepped up to the plate from all corners of America: Amy Shay, Anne Hein-Pullen, Judi Held, Shayne Hoffman, and Deborah Tasnadi (Suprak) "The Librarian," for your proofreading, pre-edits, typing and research and to Mike and Christine Johnson, Michael Olson, and Scott Siegrist for your design efforts, ideas and photography. Many thanks to Scott Pullen, my personal computer "guru" who help me out of countless jams.

I truly cannot thank each of you enough for each spice you contributed to my dream.

Chef Tory Miller

Tory Miller, Executive Chef & Co-Proprietor of L'Etoile Restaurant in Madison, Wisconsin, is passionate about delicious food, which starts with exquisite ingredients. Tory's culinary creations begin with locally grown, sustainable and organic ingredients cultivated by numerous Wisconsin farmers. Tory grew up in the restaurant industry with his sister and business partner, Traci Miller. Tory and Traci developed a passion for food and for the business at a young age. They share many wonderful memories of working in the kitchen and waiting tables while surrounded by their family. For both Tory and Traci, good food has always been a way of sharing love with family and friends; this association is one of the reasons Tory was interested in becoming a part of this book.

Tory took his early passion for food to the French Culinary Institute, where he graduated second in his class. This naturally led to jobs at several high-end restaurants in New York, including Eleven Madison Park and Judson Grill, before he arrived at L'Etoile to work as Odessa Piper's Chef de Cuisine. Now, as the Executive Chef for L'Etoile, Tory enjoys making delicious food and using L'Etoile as a focal point for supporting Wisconsin farmers and the sustainable agriculture movement on a local, regional, and national level.

L'Etoile Restaurant is nationally acclaimed for its cuisine and its dedication to supporting local farmers and sustainable agriculture. L'Etoile was ranked number fourteen in the nation by Gourmet Magazine and was awarded four stars by restaurant critic Dennis Getto. Founded in 1976, L'Etoile has been a Wisconsin treasure on the Capitol Square for thirty years and is a must visit if you find yourselves in Madison.

Since they started working together at L'Etoile, Tory and Traci have been dreaming of setting up a fund for L'Etoile's farmers. Their hope was to create a reserve fund from which they could offer support to farmers in need, beyond L'Etoile's already strong support as a customer.

In the first year of owning L'Etoile, they witnessed farmers struggling to acquire new equipment for their sustainable farms, trying to go to school to develop business plans and learn more about sustainable techniques, and suffer huge losses due to natural disasters beyond their control. Tory and Traci are delighted that this book has provided them the opportunity to start this fund; they are committing all of the proceeds that L'Etoile may receive from this book to the L'Etoile Farmer Fund.

FOREWORD

Like most men who are probably reading this, I started out with the notion that I knew all I needed to know about romance. I thought, "I know all there is to know and there is little room for improvement."

At this moment if you're a woman reading this book, you're probably laughing or quietly thinking, "Yeah right! A man who understands romance…no way!" Well if that's what you're thinking, then you are correct. After going through this book, I realized that if I had to take a romance test, I would have failed miserably.

All I know about romance I learned in those wonderful black and white movies. To be romantic you had to be able to dance like Ginger Rogers and Fred Astaire. To be a tough yet sensitive romantic, you had to be like Humphrey Bogart and Ingrid Bergman in Casablanca. To be romantic, you had to be funny like Cary Grant was with Claudette Colbert. I got my B.S. in Romance from the television. Is there any wonder why we live in a world where there is a 57.7% divorce rate?

I thought romance was simply a matter of having these few ingredients, a repertoire if you will, to lull your partner into the mood. You know the ingredients I'm referring to: nice dinner, candlelit room, soft music, and a little dancing under the pale moonlight. I mean, what more is there to romance, right? Wrong! If fact, after reading this book, I realized I was wrong on a few things:

I thought I knew how to prepare a romantic bath. No. I knew about preparing romantic meals. Wrong! Knew about flowers? Oh, so wrong! Gift ideas? Not even close!

Romance-411 is a man's manifesto (or woman's for that matter) for understanding how to romance to a level beyond the mundane and into a ethereal state of passion and unpredictability. Each chapter contains an interplay between mental foreplay and the action steps you can take to achieve romantic ecstasy with your partner.

Doing something romantic is simply a gesture that demonstrates to your partner that you care. But romance is more than that. Achieving the 'romantic' state is, as Traci points out in this book, the relinquishment of ego. It's a state of being that has all of you focusing all your attention on your partner because romance isn't about how you make your partner feel, but how you make your partner feel about him or herself.

This subtle yet potent differentiation is the underlying theme that is woven throughout the chapters of this book.

Now I know that you're thinking that being romantic is really a matter of pleasing your partner physically. Before reading this book, I thought the same thing. But I've come to understand that achieving the romantic state can only be fully appreciated and realized when you are no longer the center of attention and all your energy, spirit, and consciousness is aimed at making your partner feel loved, honored, and appreciated.

Traci's book is almost metaphysical and existential in nature in that all the ingredients for romance, which she highlights throughout this book, are aimed at engaging and exciting your partner's most innermost, unexpressed desires. I say almost because in this book you will also find tangible ideas, strategies, and simple reminders that you can implement to help move your partner into the desired state of being romantic. Whether you're a man or a woman, you are about to discover a treasure trove of fantastic and exciting ideas on romance.

In my book, The Logic of Success, I make a bold statement that success does happen for a reason. I outline what are the necessary steps to become successful in your own right. Success isn't serendipitous; there's a logic to why some people succeed while others fail.

I will make another bold statement and tell you that romance happens for a reason. There is an inherent logic to why some people are lousy (or lazy) at romance while others have mastered the art form. Traci gives you quality tips and mental triggering mechanisms to help you become romantically successful. Enjoy the adventure.

Victor Gonzalez
Author, The Logic of Success
www.victorgonzalez.com

Dear Reader,

You are about to read a book that is very personal; the pages that follow have been uprooted from my own heart. Although I never intended to write a book about romance, I felt compelled to write this book after a two-year backpacking pilgrimage around the world. My journey began with the discovery of love's importance in my own life, however, it was after many incredible conversations with other world travellers about the importance of love and romance that I knew I had a message I needed to share. After my return, I rediscovered my stained and sun-faded notepad that bound my unsuspecting worldly "survey" on love and romance. Drawing on this inspiration, I began to write.

I wholeheartedly believe that there is something in this book for everyone. I presume (and hope) that many of you do not need a road map to create a meaningful and romantic evening with your partner and are simply snooping around for some new ideas to showcase on your own. However, for those of you who are out of practice or less confident in the area of romance, this book also has formatted steps laid out with a "turn-left-here" concept that will help you get started. Whatever your romantic ability, I strongly encourage and challenge each of you to be as creative, authentic, and resourceful, as you can in planning your own romantic time with your loved one. Remember, for many romance-starved partners, it's not the cost, experience, or presentation of a romantic gesture that makes an impact, but the time, intent, thought, imagination, and effort that went into making your partner feel special and appreciated that will be the heart of the memory for years to come. If you are among the few and fortunate, whose partner does surprise you with periodic romantic interludes, be sure to compliment the thoughtfulness, praise the effort, and express what the experience meant to you. If your partner really feels good about what he/she has done based on your reaction then he/she will be more apt to want to do it again!

I sincerely thank you for purchasing this book. I believe that if we each learn at least one new valuable lesson or useful piece of information in anything we read, do, or see, then it was worth our investment - be it time, effort, or expense. In writing this book for you, my hope has been that you will walk away having learned at least one new concept, idea, or slice of knowledge that will benefit your relationship. I also believe strongly in the power of tithing, and thanks to your purchase, 10% of profits will be tithed to charity each quarter.

Thank you for indirectly helping me to make a difference in the lives of those less fortunate than we are.

May your life be filled with ethereal melodies of romance,

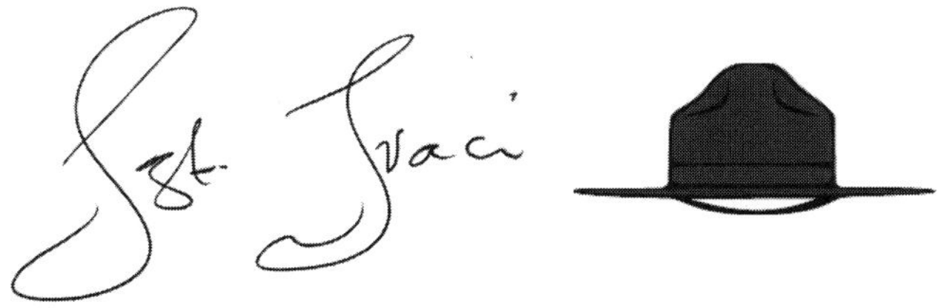

Sgt. Traci

Introduction

“It seems like the only place that romance happens before sex these days is in the dictionary.”

–Sgt. Traci

Are you romantically-challenged? You just can't seem to pull off a romantic night together? This book is designed to help you step out of your comfort zone and add a little romance and playfulness to your love life. Remember, there is no right or wrong way to be romantic, be it spontaneous or planned, playful or steamy, simple or extravagant, budgeted or exorbitant...if you feel it with your heart, it is right... follow it.

I do believe that anyone can be romantic and that being romantic is a matter of choice, and choice is a matter of priority. If there was a thousand dollar cash prize waiting for every romantic gesture we made, I believe most of us –without thought– would immediately offer random acts of romance to others. But somewhere along the line, the act of being romantic seems to have become dismally synonymous with a "chore." I am not saying that we all have to run out and erect a Taj Mahal to commemorate our beloved, but I am saying that with a 57.7% divorce rate, we could all stand to be a little more open and receptive to romance.

I know firsthand that it is easy to get caught-up in day-to-day life and become "lazy" romantically as we get stuck in our busy routines and suffer from day's end exhaustion. Yet we all make time to plan for appointments, budgets, weddings, retirement, family vacations, movies we want to see, and even what we want to wear to the Jones' party three months from now, so why not plan for intimate time with our lover? I specifically designed the "For the One I Love" Invitation concept to encourage you to schedule pre-planned "quality-time" with the one you love most. I hope you will make it a "date" and mark it on your calendar! I have also heard people complain that the "extra" money needed to pamper our sweetheart just isn't there. Yet compliments are free! We also never seem to lack enough pocket-change to support our nicotine addiction, our weekend six-pack, our daily "latte and bagel" fix, or our dream of winning it big with lottery ticket purchases. I believe that if we would spend a fraction of the amount of time, consideration, effort, and love on or for our partner as we do on and for ourselves, it would have huge pay-offs in our relationships. You can make your date evening as expensive and elaborate or as inexpensive and simple as you like. However you set it up, there is no greater gift you can give than the gift of undisturbed quality time spent together!

The ideas suggested in this book are designed to inspire your date night. You will first need to designate the time that you and your significant other will be spending together. Even if you've been together for years, plan ahead so you can both enjoy anticipating the fun that comes with going on a "date" together. Try making "date-night" a part of your weekly or monthly routine, so you'll always have something to look forward to.

I have tried to offer ideas that accommodate everyone's pocketbooks, but if you are on a strict budget, I hope you will tap into your creative resources and improvise using these ideas as a starting point. Here are just a few simple and inexpensive strategies to get you started. You see, these ideas are nothing "new." They are not out of reach, nor do they require that much "extra" time out of your busy day. WHY? Because you have to eat, you have to sleep, you have to shower, and it is recommended that you should exercise (at least once in a while). So why not make your everyday necessities ROMANTIC - simply by including your partner and he/she doesn't even have to know your "kill two birds with one stone" strategy! Try ...

- Setting the alarm clock a little earlier than normal and start the morning with bagels and tea together

- Rather than hitting the snooze button, snuggle for five minutes

- Meet at lunchtime for a picnic in the park or outdoors on a nearby patch of grass. If the weather isn't cooperative, just brown bag it in the break room

- Meet after work at a restaurant for a refreshing beverage and some pupus (Hawaiian for appetizers)

- Mutually pre-arrange for the day off or cash in one of your "sick" day chips from work and spend quality time together

- Order in and eat in bed or in front of your favorite movie

- If you usually dine out, prepare a home-cooked meal; use your best stemware, crystal, fine China, and linens

- Share dessert

- Enjoy an after dinner stroll together while having a great conversation, getting fresh air, and burning off a few calories
- Take a bath or shower together; take turns washing each other
- Retire to bed early and take turns pampering one another with sensual massages
- Have a camp out in the backyard beneath the stars
- Read your partner his/her favorite bedtime story from when he/she was a kid

So, now that I bought this book what do I do?

First, have fun with it! Familiarize yourself with the ideas these pages contain. You will find chapters with ideas for themed evenings, sensual bath recipes, delicious meals, and more. Drawing on this inspiration, determine what your partner would most appreciate and, more importantly, what you feel comfortable with, confident about, and capable of emulating with the fewest glitches. Then fill out an "Invitation" asking your loved one to join you for a special evening; you can tell him/her what awaits, or you can keep the plan a surprise. Once you have decided what you want to do for your loved one, custom design a "Romance Plan" or if you are truly romantically challenged, follow your romantic selection, step-by-step and you are on your way to a sensual, romantic, and memorable evening with your lover.

Romance Basics

“Love is two souls engaged in destiny.”

–Sgt. Traci

What is Romance? Romance is an ongoing love affair. Romance is all about soulfulness, imagination, thought, effort, and time devoted to making that special someone feel truly special. While it does take effort, time, and sometimes expense to pull off an exquisite romantic evening, what it all boils down to is a "labor of love." I personally enjoy every moment spent setting the stage for a romantic evening just as much as I enjoy seeing the joy in my partner's face while we share the experience. It is about making an extra effort and taking the time to make your significant other feel special, desired, sexy, and admired. It all comes down to the quality of the time shared together, not how deeply you reached into your pocket book.

Romance is especially beautiful in the little things and across time; it is often the little things that end up mattering most. There is romance in gentle approaches, in silent glances, and tender touches. Take time to hug long, deep, and often. Meaningful "I'm off to work now" kisses should last at least seven to ten seconds. Pay attention and listen to the wants, needs, and desires of your partner. Be open and supportive of growth and change in your partner as well as in your relationship. It is easy to criticize. Make a conscious effort to compliment your partner. Tell him something "good" about himself and "uptalk" him behind his back. Make romance a habit. Develop your natural instincts with repetition to make romantic gestures seem almost effortless.

Being romantic is more than something you do, it is something you feel. Romantic feelings stem from love and passion; romantic feelings create a constant desire to please, invent, and detail verse, deeds, and gestures concerning your lover. Romantic feelings are like a fire that burns deeply within your soul that makes you want to share with, give to, and be your very best for your lover. When romantic emotions swell inside you, you will find that they heighten every experience you have with your lover.

I believe that if we could feel what we impart to others, there would be a lot less conflict and a lot more loving in this world. But since we cannot directly feel the effect and impact of our words and actions, it is up to us to take the initiative to put our best foot forward and commit to treating our partner (and our friends, family, and neighbors) the way that we want and desire to be treated.

Intimacy has little to do with physical or sexual acts and all the things that we think are related to it. Intimacy is an emotion, not an act. It is a feeling, not a sensation. It is a touch without contact. Intimacy reveals exactly what it reflects, our inner essence...Intimacy = "Into-me-see." It is the total surrender of your ego. It is not always easy to stand in front of another, even the one you love, and be totally and completely vulnerable.

While some of these sensationalized ideas are flattering and appealing to the person receiving this prized potpourri of affection, there is really something to be said about true intimacy between lovers and the bond created from being emotionally naked in front of one another.

True intimacy is a process. It is a journey, not a destination. It is not in knowing every little "thing" about your partner, but rather, it's a layered maturation of knowing and embracing the genesis of your partner's needs, strengths, fears, weaknesses, vulnerabilities, goals, yearnings, and esteem. With true intimacy is born an understanding of how you can better celebrate, serve, and honor your partner's inner treasure - his or her inner self. True intimacy is ultimately about living your best life, so in turn you can uplift your partner to live his.

To firmly establish intimacy in your relationship, you should express yourself often and stay connected with your partner through touch (holding hands, snuggling, kisses), eye contact (anytime you are talking, flirtatious glances), playful interactions, sweet gestures, kind words, loving deeds, gift giving, frequent compliments, and most importantly of all, really listening to each other. Integrate the purity of spiritual and emotional love with the ecstasy of physical love by living the "100/100" rule rather than the overused "50/50" rule of giving in and to your relationship. Can you imagine what you would experience if you each contributed 100% of yourselves to your relationship rather than just your expected share of "50%"? The feeling is absolutely celestial!

We all possess an innate need for a sense of belonging, adequacy, purpose, and competence in our lives. We all seek a sense of validation and worth in the eyes of someone we love. Be that "someone" for your partner by nurturing those needs and taking steps towards fulfilling them. Your efforts will help to establish a relationship where your needs can be equally nurtured and fulfilled. Don't hesitate to talk about your wants and needs together; it is much easier to take care of each other if you know how you each feel and what creates a sense of belonging and adequacy for each of you.

All of these thoughts are important for long-term romance and intimacy in your relationship; however, for tonight, start simply by remembering that it is not about you. For this night, live to serve and please only your partner. Understand that romance is not synonymous with sex (but adding romance to your relationship is likely to earn you some real passion points). Emotional intimacy can be equally as powerful and stimulating as sexual intimacy.

You know what romance is in your mind, but do you know what romance is for your partner? Does your partner know what romance is for you? To further enhance your relationship and to satisfy each other's desires, sit down together and write out ten things that you each feel are romantic. When you are finished, give your partner the piece of paper. You may gain some new insight or simply be reminded of a small gem that was forgotten over the years. Whatever the case may be, take that piece of paper and pick a day, any day, and surprise your partner with romance "their" way!

Here are some examples to get you started:

Romance to me is when you show me affection and we stay in bed snuggling for an extra fifteen minutes on a hectic week day morning rather than hitting the snooze button.

Romance to me is when you give me an impromptu neck massage while I am washing dishes after dinner.

Romance to me is the enthusiastic greeting you give me whenever I come home.

Romance to me is an after dinner walk through the neighborhood, whether it is springtime and the flowers are blooming or winter and we are walking through the snow.

Romance to me is ordering take-out, turning off the phone, and eating dinner on the couch watching a movie.

Romance to me is sitting down together after work with a cup of tea or a glass of wine and just talking.

Romance to me is snuggling and not needing to talk, just enjoying being together.

General Tips for Creating a Romantic Atmosphere:

• Set the mood with soft music and aromatic scents exorbitant that best suit and complement your occasion and your partner. Take extra measures to ensure that your atmosphere and person are clean and smells appealing: skin, hair, clothing, shoes, breath, and sheets.

• Candles are synonymous with romance. The power of candlelight en masse is more than a vision; it evokes a feeling. You can never have too many candles because lighting plays a major role in setting the mood for a warm and seductive intimate interlude. Candlelight is probably the most flattering source of illumination for a "romantic" evening, although track-lighting or lights that are controlled by a dimmer switch can set a lovely mood too.

• Satin, silk, chenille, and velvet are some of the textures of romance. Dress your person, surroundings, and your bed for the occasion. You can add a different type of atmosphere with a bear skin, sheepskin, or Persian rug (preferably imitation animal skin) If you do not have or cannot afford articles made from these materials, choose some thing that is soft and clean to set your stage. The most important thing in regard to texture is that the area be soft on the skin, clean and inviting. You can set a very romantic stage with clean cotton sheets, candles, lotion, and a single flower nearby.

• Keep in mind that men tend to be more "conquering", visual and physical, while women tend to be more nurturing, emotional and sensual. Honor and respect each other's remarkable genetic makeup. There is an old saying that says "Keep Mamma Bear happy and everyone is happy." Men, heed the wisdom of the ages. You are more likely to have a fulfilling sex life if you continually satisfy the romantic and emotional needs of your partner. Start as simply as talking or listening more, and ladies, touch and "dress" the part more often! Simple little ripples of change can have a tidal wave effect on your relationship.

• Always be prepared. The best time to be romantic is anytime at all. Keep a bedside collection of all of your favorite romance essentials.

Stories that Inspired the Book:

“One moment of romance between lovers melts the ills of an entire day.”

–Sgt. Traci

After my travel-companion (my best friend, Amy) returned to America, I ventured on solo or joined in with tour groups through another fifteen countries; perhaps it was out of eighteen hour train jaunt boredom or the fact that I simply longed to feel loved and accepted by another human being - two worlds away from home and away from everything familiar and comforting to me. Whatever the reason, I began to have a new kind of conversation with the people I was meeting rather than the same old shallow talk about the weather, our professions, and tourist recommendations. There in the third world of simplicity, I had one of many revelations on my journey of discovery; I got in touch with the raw nakedness of the heart of humanity. Despite our differences in language, culture, religious beliefs, and the worlds and wars between us, we all have a common denominator that cements us together like links in a chain wrapped around our only Mother (Earth), the universal bond of love. Love was something we could all relate to, easily converse about and heartily agree upon. It seemed that in a single moment, we went from not being able to speak each other's language to developing genuine connections with one another.

As I wallowed in the emptiness of my own heart, I began asking people from all corners of the world what love meant to them. I asked them what gave their relationships the strength to prevail or what caused them to fail. I was surprised at how willing most people were to open up to a complete stranger. I heard great love stories and disasters alike. The responses were varied, sometimes simple, sometimes complex. Friendship, respect, truth, honesty, romance, feeling desired and appreciated were all top contenders for why marriages/relationships thrived and lack of those attributes were among the top reasons they failed. I agree that each and every one of those aspects is a necessary and important factor for sustaining a successful and fulfilling relationship; I would also contend that romance is an often under-rated element that adds strength to all relationships. The art of romance is a true spice of life and is a great way to maintain a harmonious and fruitful relationship as well as a great resuscitation device to aid in reviving a failing one.

As I ventured on and the superficial conversations turned to ones of love and complete strangers turned to "friends," I pressed the conversations a little further to ask about romance. I started asking,

"What is the most romantic thing that you have ever done for someone?" and "What is the most romantic thing that anyone has ever done for you?" While there were numerous really beautiful and inventive stories, I was truly surprised to learn that for most people the standard "candlelight dinner" routine was the hands-down winner for the most romantic evening. While I agree candlelight dinners can be alluring, soft, elegant, and meaningful, they are not the be-all, end-all in the arena of romance and in my home, they are not the exception; they are the rule. In sharing this book with you, I hope to broaden your romantic horizon by furnishing you with a rich storehouse of fresh and inspiring ideas. However, I know that the true wellspring of romance comes from inside of each of us, and in order to have a happy and healthy relationship, you must first have a happy and healthy "you." Here are just a few examples of the stories that inspired this book.

My curiosity about the world of romantic indulgence began while I was seeing the sights of America prior to departing for my around the world backpacking adventure. I was in Texas for about fifteen weeks exploring the wonders of that beautiful state. I was pulled over en route to a service station to have a stripped screw on my license plate removed so I could replace my newly expired out-of-state plates with current plates. So there I was driving with one newly placed Wisconsin plate on the back of the car and one expired plate from Colorado on the front of the car in a vehicle that was registered to my travel-companion while I was driving with my Hawaiian driver's license. I thought I was in big trouble when a second squad car arrived to the scene, but to my surprise, believe this or not, I was given a personal escort to the service station! No ticket was issued. Instead, the officer and I became friends. He and his K-9 dog frequently stopped at my roommate's and my interim housing location for cookies and conversation during his patrol breaks.

One day, we got onto the subject of romance; he was a self-proclaimed romantic who prided himself on his Prince Charming ways. He had really built up his romantic escapades, and I was beginning to think that I was about to be romantically impressed, which doesn't happen very often. He boasted in a "bet ya can't top that one" fashion that he really "pulled out all the stops" and took romance to new levels. Finally, I couldn't take the suspense anymore, and I asked him if he would describe his most romantic evening ever. He said that not only did he cook his sweetie her favorite meal, but he had really gone the extra mile and bought some wine, played soft music, and that he didn't even stop at dimming the lights...he had even gone so far as to light candles for her during dinner! Sometimes I admired that candlelight dinner simplicity, and other times I pitied it. I soon left Texas and was on to the next place, but the impression made from that "taking romance to new levels" conversation never left my mind.

One fella had his heart in the right place when he tried implementing his first romantic evening for his girlfriend. He prepared her favorite meal complete with background mood music, dimmed the lights low, lit some scented candles and poured his sweetie her favorite glass of wine. They were engaged in deep heartfelt conversation when suddenly the curtains and couch caught fire from the unattended candle that was inadvertently placed too close to the window, subsequently ruining the evening. This poor guy was so devastated that he vowed to never entertain a romantic evening again.

While this next story was told to me secondhand, it is still my favorite. Frank had done some favors for one of his associates, Mary. So she thought she'd do something nice in return and decided to give him one of the expensive themed romantic gift-basket "experiences" that she sells. She selected the "Breakfast in Bed Experience" with all the makings from the bed table and mugs of gourmet tea & coffee to biscotti with jam and "mood" music. She assumed that Frank would present "Breakfast in Bed" to his wife and share in a morning of romance and togetherness. But rather than setting the stage and surprising his wife with "Breakfast in Bed" (and earning himself some real "passion points") Frank instead elected to holler to his wife that there was something for her on the counter... there sat the sealed romantic "Breakfast in Bed Experience" for her on the sink top...when she said, "What's this?" He hollered back, "It's from Mary!"

On a lighter note, I met a number of couples who had gone their separate ways from the "love of their life" and then at a later point in their lives, had rekindled their romance and re-married. Many had been married, had children, got divorced, and then married the "love of their life" in the end - after all. One couple I met in South Africa was on their honeymoon. It was their third marriage…to each other! They said they simply couldn't live without each other.

I was especially moved by the story of the couple whose photograph I took at the Pyramids in Egypt. They were high school sweethearts who were deeply in love. Sadly, he was called away to serve his country overseas. When he returned to America, he learned that his love had met someone new. Both ended up marrying other people and raised families. Eventually, both of their spouses had died. They met again at their fortieth high school class reunion and knew instantly that they were meant to spend the remainder of their lives together; they both sold their homes in different states, agreed on a new place of residence- someplace neither of them had ever been before and had always dreamed of visiting, met there and married one week later. He said, "There's just something about your first love. I always knew that we were meant to be - but I didn't know when and I didn't know how, I just knew!" He went on to say that while he was very happy with his life and the family he shared with his deceased wife, he had often thought and wondered about his "first love" and what might have been. He said that she was the unconscious ache in his heart that never went away until the day they re-connected! What a beautiful, inspiring, and powerful story of love.

Here is one lucky woman who is fortunate enough to be married to a true romantic, even thirty-four years into their marriage. She says, "In the early years of our courtship, we dreamed about traveling to Australia. We actually chose 'Waltzing Matilda' as our wedding recessional song. It was our promise to each other. Sister Ancele, the organist at our wedding, made it sound like Bach, but we knew. It wasn't until January of 2005, some thirty-three years after our marriage, that we were finally able to make that trip. In addition to the usual tourist highlights, we were visiting libraries, and my husband was presenting a workshop in Adelaide for the Australian Library Association. Dr. Al Bundy, who coordinated the library session and facilitated our library visits, invited us to attend his daughter's wedding, which coincided with the final evening of our trip. The third day of the trip was my 54th birthday. We were hiking in the Blue Mountains. As we reached the blue pool, a truly lovely place, my husband pulled my birthday gift out of his pack. It was a small pewter box with Waltzing Matilda and the date of our trip engraved on the lid. Inside was a small voice-activated recorder. He had gone back to Sister Ancele and had her record all of the music from our wedding. We waltzed teary-eyed beside the blue pool. Weeks later as our trip was coming to a close, there was another surprise in store. Dr. Al Bundy introduced us to the wedding guests as his friends from the states. After the traditional wedding dances, the assembled guests serenaded us with Waltzing Matilda as we took to the floor for our own special waltz. We were able to record it on the same recorder. I will treasure this gift and these memories forever."

There are so many beautiful stories of love and romance in the world. I hope that this book will inspire you to create many more of them for yourself and your loved one.

Time for Romance

"True vulnerability is the strength to stand emotionally naked in front of the person you love and ask them to love you in spite of what they see."

–Sgt. Traci

Any time is a good time for romance. Whether you have five minutes or an entire evening set aside, making the effort to do something thoughtful for your loved one will make an impression. This section of the book covers ways to court your lover using romantically themed ideas, from breakfast in bed to elaborate dinner dates.

Getting Started:

Look over your plans for the evening of your choice and make a list of all the materials you will need.

Gather your materials either from around the house or go shopping. If you need to shop and are on a budget, try stopping at yard sales, secondhand stores/thrift shops, and the Dollar Store to find anything you need for your date.

If your plans involve going out, try purchasing an Entertainment Book. (I never leave home without one!) This mammoth coupon savings book offers buy one, get one free coupons for meals and entertainment and various travel discounts. If you are going on vacation, order an Entertainment Book for your destination state and have it delivered to your home prior to your departure. My family collectively saved more than $2,000 while visiting me in Hawaii for two weeks, using the Hawaii Entertainment Book that they ordered for $35. Many local organizations sell Entertainment Books as fundraisers offering you the opportunity to support a charitable cause, and at the same time, get out and explore new places that you might not otherwise have tried. www.entertainmentbook.com.

Once you have gathered everything you need, take time to set the stage and the mood. Appropriately themed music always enhances a romantic affair; you should pick something you know your loved one will enjoy. Candle lighting also enhances romantic evenings, and I recommend using them whenever possible. Although since I met a man during my world travels who had a romantic event turn into a disaster thanks to candles, I would like to take a moment to include some tips on candle safety.

Candle Care Reminders and Tips

• All candles are a potential fire hazard. After all, they represent an open flame in your home. This section is intended to help you get the most enjoyment from your candles; for more information, please visit www.candlekitchen.com & www.stormsong.org, who kindly provided these safety tips.

• Candles burn more quickly in warmer weather than in colder weather. By storing candles in the refrigerator, you can promote slower burning all year-round. Keep burning.

• Always keep lit candles out of the reach of children and pets and away from flammable items. Never leave a burning candle unattended! Keep the wick trimmed to ¼" for best burning. Votives and 1 -1/2"x 6" Altar Pillars must be used in holders which are large enough to catch and contain the melt pool.

• Plan to burn a candle for at least 1 hour for every inch of diameter or until a pool of melted wax covers the top of the candle. (This is especially important on larger candles such as 3x6 pillars and three-wick candles or you'll end up with a hole burned straight down the middle of the candle.) Burning a candle for more than 1 hour past diameter is not advised as the melt pool can release itself. (Messy!)

• The wick is designed to produce a small black carbon cap at the top of the wick as it burns. This is normal and helps radiate heat to the edge of the candle. You should not trim the wick or touch it while it's cold. Immediately after extinguishing the flame is the best time to remove carbon deposits or other foreign materials from the liquid wax. Once you extinguish the flame from a votive candle, you should center the wick before the wax solidifies to prevent the flame from getting close to the edge and cracking the glass votive container during your next burn.

• Pop any leftover wax out of the jar or votive holder and place it in a tart-burner. Light a tea candle underneath it, and it releases a nice scent for many hours, just like fragrance tarts.

• If you spill wax on the carpet or fabric, the easiest way to remove the wax is by placing a paper towel or a brown grocery bag over it. Place a warm iron on top of the paper towel or bag and the heat will cause the wax to soak up and onto the paper towel or bag. To remove candle wax from glass, place the glass piece in your freezer for about 10-15 minutes. The wax should pop right off. You can also fill a votive cup with no more than ¼" of water before placing your votive in the holder to make wax easier to remove. Another method for removing votive candles from their holders is to put the container in a sink of hot water. Let it sit for a couple of minutes and then hold it upside down and it should pop right out.

• Herbs, flowers, and spices are flammable and may spark and cause the flame to burn higher than it would normally. Please use extra caution when burning these candles and move herbs and flowers out of the flame to keep the candle from burning too fast.

• Light candles when you are dusting your home. The dust will be attracted to and burn up in the candle flame as it tries to settle back down. (Same goes for cigarette and cigar smoke too.)

• Rub your candles with vegetable oil to remove fingerprints, smudges, and small scratches.

Breakfast in Bed

The morning is a beautiful time for romance! It is often overlooked in favor of the more traditional evening candlelit dinner; however, romance in the morning is a great way to start the day.

Morning Ingredients:

Coffee, tea, or freshly squeezed juice

Copy of the morning newspaper or favorite reading material

Tray or sturdy surface to present the breakfast on

A napkin and a kitchen towel for the tray (always good to keep handy in case the tray gets bumped and you have minor beverage spills)

A single flower in a vase

Bell

Daily supply of vitamins

Breakfast Ingredients, make up your own or follow our Chef's suggestions

Reminders:

• Make sure you have cleared the calendar and made alternate plans for the children or are prepared to keep them busy so that nothing disturbs your partner's morning.

• Place the bell by your partner's side of the bed the night before, pre-stow his/her favorite reading material nearby, and have his/her favorite movie, with alternate selections on hand, ready for the VCR/ DVD player.

• Before you greet your partner in the morning, brush your teeth and make sure your breath is fresh and you are ready with a smile.

• The evening prior to your partner's breakfast in bed, present him/ her with an invitation to explain what your romantic plan involves.

• The evening prior to your partner's breakfast in bed, present him/her with an invitation to explain what your romantic plan involves.

Here is a sample invitation you might want to consider:

For the One I Love

"In the morning you will have the opportunity to "sleep-in" undisturbed or simply laze in bed, snuggled up with your favorite novel or engrossed in your favorite movie. Regardless of how you choose to spend the morning, it is all yours."

When you awake in the morning, be sure to slip out of bed and out of the room silently. Let your partner rest and relax in the bedroom until he/she asks you to come in by ringing the bell. Leave a card on the pillow next to your lover to let him/her know that you will return when you are called in.

For the One I Love

"When you are ready for breakfast, please ring the bell, and your personal concierge will greet you with a smile and a custom designed breakfast menu."

When your lover has asked you to return to the room, greet him/her sweetly and welcome him/her to your Bed and Breakfast. Then present the menu and ask your partner to look it over. As the concierge, feel free to mention any chef recommendations or house specialties before you take your partner's order. Be sure to give your lover an approximate time that breakfast will be served, then leave him/her alone to relax and get cooking.

Sample Menu

Breakfast in Bed for My Love

Entrée Choices

Pancakes
French Toast
Waffles
Eggs Any Style
Oatmeal
Cereal
Toast or Bagel
Fresh Fruit & Yogurt

Side Dishes

Bacon
Sausage
Hash Browns

Beverage Choices

Coffee
Tea
Milk
Juice

When breakfast is ready, serve it on a tray with another note:

For the One I Love

"After breakfast and at your own lazy pace, ring the bell, and your personal concierge will promptly clear your tray."

If you have invited your loved one to enjoy a luxurious bath after breakfast, you should prepare it now! If not, feel free to sit with your loved one and feed him/her, eat with him/her, or just snuggle once the food has been cleared away. Whatever your loved one wants to do with the rest of the morning, you should do your best to accommodate those wishes.

Welcome to Roman Times

This evening you and your loved one return to "Roman Times" for a picnic in the moonlight followed by a Roman bath. The ambience will be set with torchlight in your backyard (or any other area appropriate for a picnic) and enhanced by your matching togas.

Roman-tic Evening Ingredients:

Two togas

Tiki torch or candles

Goblets or glasses

Small grill or makings for a safe campfire

Blanket

Classical music or Poem

Dinner Ingredients and Skewers

Bath Ingredients

How to Make a Toga:

By Kathleen Colussy, the Art Institute of Fort Lauderdale
www.ComputersandFashion.com or www.aifl.edu

There are two simple variations on how to make a toga. The first uses one rectangle of fabric, at least five yards long, which is wrapped around the body. The second is constructed from a semicircle cut from fabric the size of a double or a queen-size sheet. It is important to note, that more or less fabric may be required based on the size of the lady or gentleman who will be sporting the toga and any desire for more or less coverage based on personal aesthetic and functional preferences.

Supplies:

Fabric, either an old sheet (secondhand is inexpensive) or several yards of muslin or other cool looking material

Sewing threads to match, Velcro or iron-on tape

Several large safety pins

One large brooch to fasten at the shoulder (optional)

Directions:

For best results, you should measure your fabric before cutting to make sure that you have enough. You will need a piece approximately 6 yards long and 2 yards wide. If time does not allow for measuring and cutting a length of fabric, you can also fold a large bed sheet on the diagonal and use that. When using sheets you may want to cut into the top center of the semicircle, cutting about 1/4 to 1/3 of the way into center of the fabric. This cut will help the sheet drape successfully around the body.

If you wish to construct a finished hem where the fabric has been cut, you can, but this step is completely optional. If you are an overachiever, try sewing a 1-inch hem or use iron-on tape to secure a seam. (Velcro or heavy double sided tape will also work for a quick fix.)

The best way to drape the fabric correctly is to place the fabric from the back of the body over one shoulder. From here there are several variations. Version 1: bring the remaining fabric around the waist and up over the opposite shoulder or opt to pin the remaining fabric to secure the garment. Version 2: take the remaining fabric and wrap several times around the body. (See Illustration on the next page for variations)

Finally, once you have the amount of draping and folding you are comfortable with, take the excess fabric and throw it over either the right or left shoulder, and fasten with a safety pin or brooch.

Note that once the fabric has been secured, the excess should fall from the waist down and reach approximately to the knees or mid calf. If the trailing fabric is too long, make some additional folds in the cloth.

Men should wear some sort of shorts because the toga will later be fastened to what is worn under the toga.

Accessorize with sandals, armband, laurel leaf crowns, plastic shields and swords, and voila, you're back in the Roman Times!

For all of your themed evening essentials: www.anytimecostumes.com & www.allcostumes.com.

Invite your loved one to join you for an evening where:

For the One I Love

"We will roast skewers of fowl, eat with our hands, drink wine from antique goblets, and recite century old poetry."

Serve your favorite bread, soup, skewers and dessert and eat them all with your hands. Even your soup is not to be eaten with a spoon but to be consumed from the bowl. Corn bread, vegetable soup and variety kabobs make for a delicious Roman Times feast. For the kabobs, simply add your favorite vegetables, potatoes, fruits and meats to a skewer and roast on an open fire or grill. When serving, refer to it as roasted "dragon tail" meat or skinned "fowl."

Set up your picnic-style feasting ground and make it fit for an emperor. Lay down blankets and pillows for lounging and surround the area with torches and candlelight.

Serve drinks in old goblets available at most local "party shops" or purchase online at the following web sites:
www.4fun.parties.com or www.anytimecostumes.com.

If you really want to get into theme and be semi-authentic with recipes and prop ideas, download an e-book for $9.95.
www.questexperiences.com.

Print out a free century old classic poem or write one of your own. Keep it close by so when the right time comes, you can recite it to your sweetie.
www.theromantic.com.

Hold each other close underneath the wondrous stars and dream of your future together or reminisce over past memories. Offer a compliment and tell your love how much he/she means to you. Or try wishing on a star together.

Welcome to the Big City

The city's finest is on the menu for romance this evening with dinner, wine, candlelight, and dancing.

Big City Ingredients:

Formal attire for you and your loved one

Formally set table: tablecloth, flowers, candles, best dishes, etc.

Dinner Ingredients (or Reservations at a restaurant of your choosing)

Dancing area and music

Decorations (for the fireplace, pillows, candles, etc.)

Any items for after dinner (massage oil & towels or board game pieces)

This evening, you are inviting your loved one to join you for a night on the town, so start with a formal invitation to your lover; a nice touch would be to send it in the mail. If you prefer not to mail it, you can simply slip the invitation into his or her briefcase or purse, or (my least favorite option) send an invitation style e-mail. However you deliver the message, set the date and time, along with the mood.

For the One I Love

"A table for two in the living room is where an elegant dinner by a crackling fire awaits us; we will sip wine and dance cheek to cheek in the "big city" tonight."

I once inspired a friend to come over and play chef and waiter. He showed up in a tuxedo, spoke no words, and cooked for us his specialty steak and lobster dinner. He escorted us to our table-for-two, served our meal and beverages, and refreshed our wine with a strategically placed towel over his arm for true waiter effect. He kindly cleaned up his mess and silently slipped out the back door. Although my friend's gift was extremely selfless, you too may have a friend who would be happy to offer this service to you and your loved one, in exchange for an evening where you played chef and waiter for him/her.

Tips for your Big City Date:

• When you meet your love for your date, greet him/her with an elegant kiss to his/her hand. (Remember, the proper way to kiss a hand is to lower your head to the hand; never raise the hand to meet your lips.) Before you begin your date, don't forget to tell him/her how wonderful he/she looks tonight.

• Create your evening's dinner menu using recipes from this book, or only using your sweetheart's favorite dishes, or recreate the dish he/she ordered on your first date, or serve the dinner you shared on your wedding day.

• Don't forget to warm your dinner plates in the oven at 150 degrees for fifteen minutes prior to serving dinner. (Check to assure they are warmed and not scorching hot as oven temperatures can fluctuate.)

• Serve your meal with a garnish to enhance the elegance of the plate.

• Set your table for two with your finest linen and dust off your best dishes. Dinner may be on your patio, in your living room, or, my personal favorite, on a rooftop overlooking the city.

• Dress in your best outfit as if you were going out on your first date again.

• A soft crackling fire enhances any romantic occasion. Build a fire in your fireplace, fire pit, or small grill. If you do not have one, create your own! Buy a fireplace video and play it on TV or place a cardboard cutout "wax catcher" on the floor and strategically place a sequence of three tiers of multi-height candles to act as a makeshift fireplace. In one of my best improvisations, I took a large-sized cardboard box, turned it upside-down, pushed it against a wall and decorated it to make it look like a stone fireplace. I cut out a large square to look like the fireplace opening, I poked venting holes in the top of the box and placed about thirty tea candles inside. If you plan to mimic this set up, make sure you use small, self-contained candles to keep a controlled flame.

• Enhance your evening with your favorite love songs or classical music.

This evening's theme has many possible permutations. Therefore, this section is set up for you to choose your own adventure. The options for where you eat, what you eat, and what entertainment you choose after dinner are practically endless. I hope you will have fun with the many suggestions I am about to put on the table, and that you choose to explore the ones that are right for you and your loved one.

Dinner Options:

Set out a variety of wines on your cocktail table and conduct your own wine tasting.

Personalize your dessert! Buy a tube of cake decorating gel at the grocery store and draw your initials into a heart on your dessert or write a love message on it.

Eat out at a favorite restaurant and recruit the help of a friend or florist to have flowers or a small gift delivered to your dinner table. At many fine dining restaurants you can make arrangements with the maitre d` of the restaurant ahead of time or pretend to sneak away to the rest room and make the arrangements at that time.

Whatever you choose to do during dinner, as the meal finishes, find an opportunity to pass another invitation to your lover inviting him/her to the conclusion of your evening. The invitation should allude to your plans, whatever they may be. One possibility, for example, might be:

For the One I Love

"Later, we will retreat to a floor of a hundred pillows, where you will be spoon-fed fresh New York-style Cheese Cake."

Evening Entertainment Options:

Slow dance cheek-to-cheek in the living room or on the roof top, softly singing "your song" in your lover's ear. If you are musically inclined, play your instrument in a private concert.

Go for an after dinner walk or a drive to the place where you first met, proposed, made love, conceived your child, or got married. Share some dessert there instead of at home or at the restaurant. When you get home, carry your lover over the threshold as you did on your wedding day.

Get cozy at home! Gather every pillow from every room and arrange them on the floor for a plush lounging area or create a sofa bench around the perimeter of the coffee table or choose a wall to prop your pillows against to form a lounge bed.

Although I have already said this, it is worth repeating. An evening lit by candles is unbelievably romantic. Votive candles en masse are truly more than a sight to see, they create a feeling. Tea candles are relatively inexpensive and are often sold in bags of one hundred. Really light up the night by using them all.

When is the last time you told your lover how much you appreciate him/her? Have you told him lately how much he means to you? Have you ever shared your favorite memory of her, with her? Perhaps now is the time to give your love your most sincere and heartfelt compliment.

Go and refresh your lover's drink and return with dessert or some fruit if you have already had dessert. Spoon feed your sweetheart every last bite. Share a strawberry and seductively caress it around his mouth or make him steal it from your mouth with his.

Ending Your Evening with Something Extra:

End your evening by playing an adult board game. Anticipation, surprise, adventure, the delight of discovery, and playful intimacy... await you and your partner when you play An Enchanting Evening®, Fan the Flames® or Romantic Sensations® -- romantic board games that will let you develop a deeper understanding of what you both like and what you look forward to sharing in your intimate relationship. You'll expand your awareness and indulge your senses as you lovingly build anticipation, adventure, and a progression of physical intimacy. It's fun -- and the journey is just as exciting as the destination. www.timefortwo.com

If you prefer, you can end your evening with an indulgent massage. Choose a bath to start, so your love can relax while you prepare for the massage. Begin by warming up the massage blanket in the dryer and then warm the massage oil by placing it in a bucket of hot water or in the microwave (follow exact directions on the back of the bottle). You can keep the massage oil in a bucket of hot water or wrapped in a heating pad to keep it warm throughout the massage. For an added touch, place a heating pad under the blanket. This is especially nice during the winter months. If you have rose petals from the bath, use the extras to create a trail from the outside of the bathroom to the location of the massage. You can also create a pathway using candles or a favorite candy. Give the blissful indulgence of the best massage you know how to give or read a book on the art of giving a massage. You can even go as far as having a masseuse teach you the basics. Whatever you choose to do, put your heart into it.

See You at Sunset

This will be a night to treasure as you and your loved one embark on your own treasure hunt and enchanted island dinner.

Sunset Evening Ingredients:

Keepsake Box

Small Gifts to find as Treasure Pieces

Dining area set on the floor (see instructions below)

Dinner Ingredients for "Bogan Island Dinner"

Printed Story to Read

Printed Treasure Map

Island Decorations

Get a little decorative box or you can buy one at a craft store and decorate it yourself, perhaps by gluing your old movie ticket stubs, concert tickets, napkins, wine corks, photos and love-letters to it. Or make an origami box using the newspaper announcement from your engagement, wedding, or child's birth. At evening's end, this keepsake box will be filled with your little "sweet nothings" from a personalized treasure hunt. You could also buy a durable plastic container and forever encapsulate your love by making a time capsule for the two of you to bury together. To learn more about origami art, visit: www.geocities.com/marivi_2/

Instructions to make a coffer: (By Maria Victoria Garrido)

Materials:

Cover paper

Decorative paper to wrap the coffer

Rice paper to wrap the inside

1 piece of narrow ribbon

1 piece of wide ribbon (Matching color) Ribbon to decorate

A piece of fabric or wall paper

Glue

Tools: You will need a craft knife, a ruler, and a pencil.

Process:

A: 6" x 4"
B: 3.55" x 2"
C: 6" x 2"
D: 6" x 1.7"

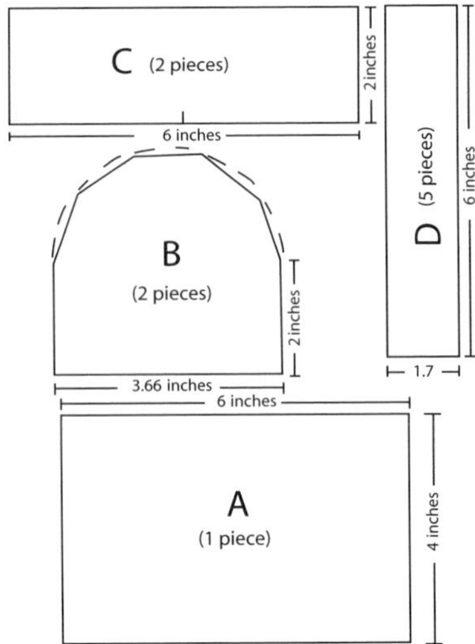

1. Cut all the pieces. Notice that pieces D (5 units) are a little longer than pieces A and C.

2. Glue all the pieces on the back side of the decorative paper spacing them 1 mm apart.

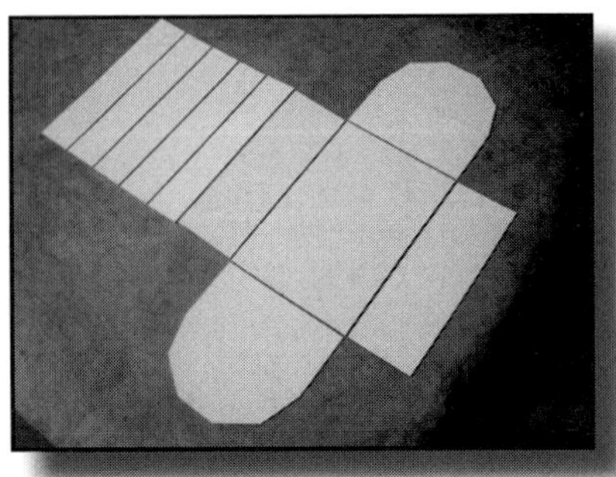

3. Measure and cut 2 cm. all around the coffer.

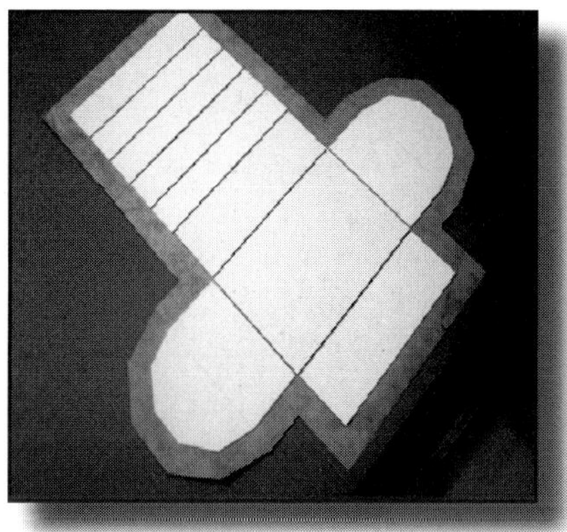

4. Cut a split toward each corner.

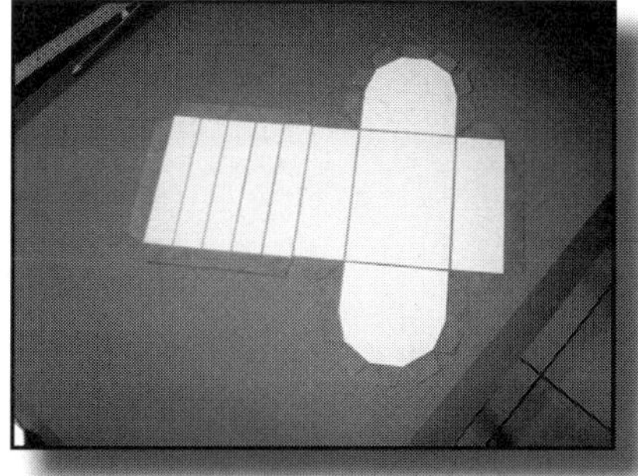

5. Apply glue on each portion to the boards, pressing firmly to ensure clean edges.

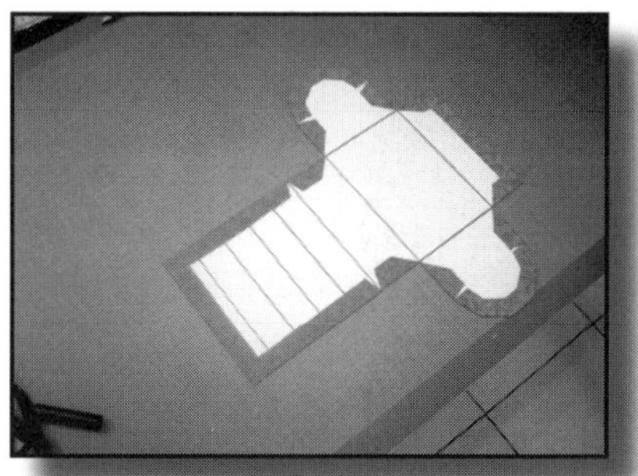

6. Measure and cut rice paper to wrap the inside of the coffer. Then glue them to the cover paper.

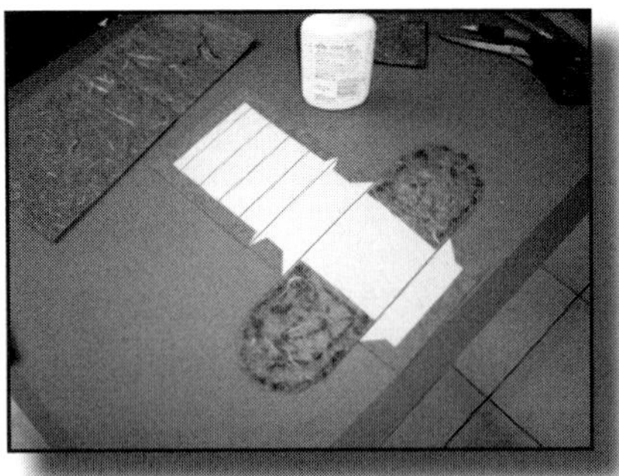
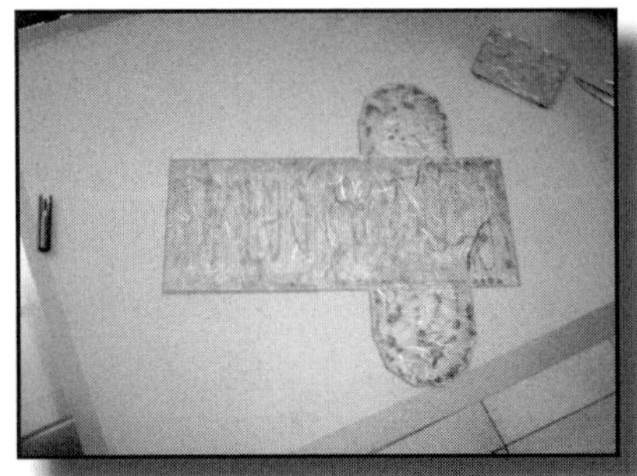

7. Cut to squares (4.5 cm side) of the fabric. Fold them in half and glue them to pieces B as shown. Let them dry.

8. Apply glue on the second half of the fabric square and joining piece B with C press firmly. Hold corner to dry firmly.

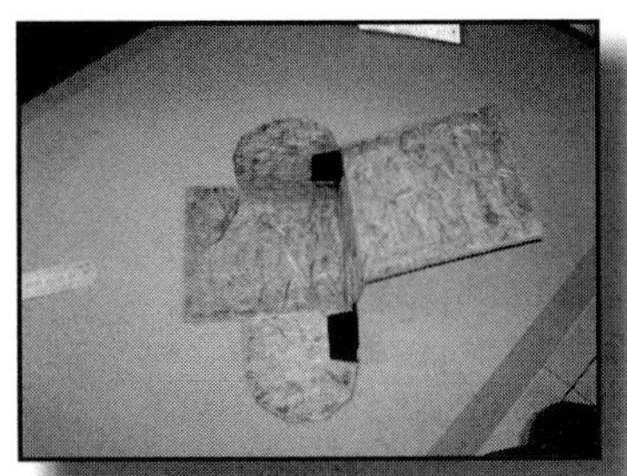

9. Once the corners are dry you have the coffer ready to decorate.

10. You can glue a narrow golden ribbon to tie better the coffer. Glue it all around the box where you like to decorate.

11. Apply glue on the bottom of the coffer and paste the thicker ribbon as shown.

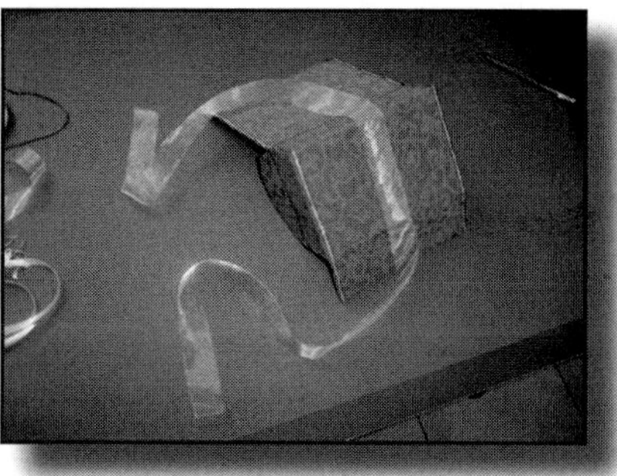

12. Apply glue and paste the thinner ribbon over the other, as shown.

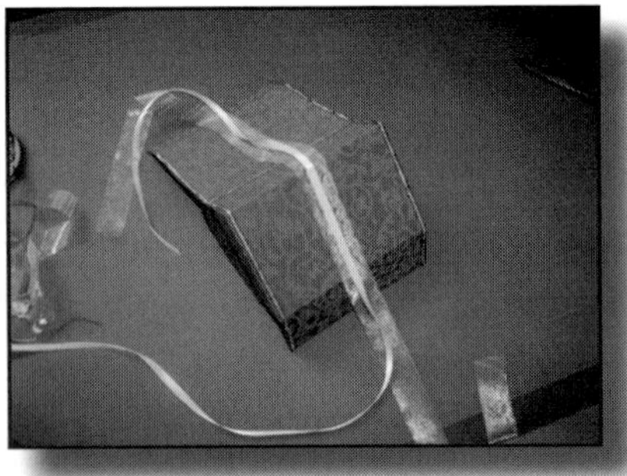

13. The coffer is finished, tie ribbon on top of it.

14. Now you can keep your memories.

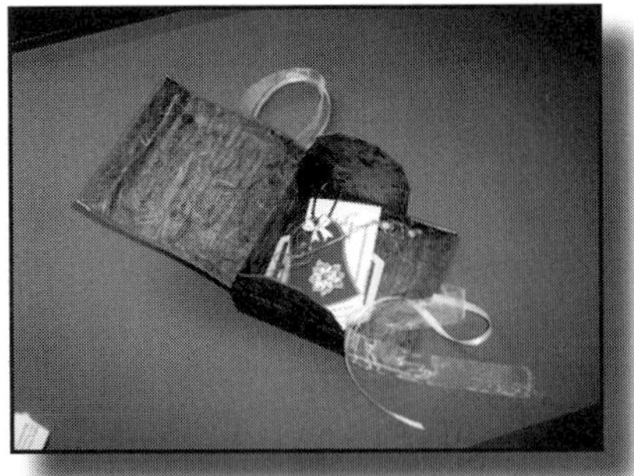

The goal is to fill the chest with the treasures you have left for your sweetheart. It is fun to start the hunt in one room with a clue to find two "treasure eggs." One egg containing a small gift and the other egg containing a clue leading to the next two eggs and so on. At the end of the hunt, have one big treasure waiting.

Treasure Hunt Gift Suggestions:

• Write a love-letter or give back an old love-letter that you received from your partner and have lovingly held onto throughout the years.

• Create a small stick man illustrated booklet entitled "Our Story" depicting how you met.

• Small individual handwritten notes of the 25 things you love most about him/her work beautifully.

• Write down some of your favorite memories, for example: how you met, your first kiss, a proposal, your wedding day, a special date, any moment in your relationship that stands out would be a lovely gift.

• The treasure could be a thimble, representing a kiss-think Peter Pan! Maybe it's a collectible thimble that might say Florida, as a clue that you are taking your partner to Disney World.

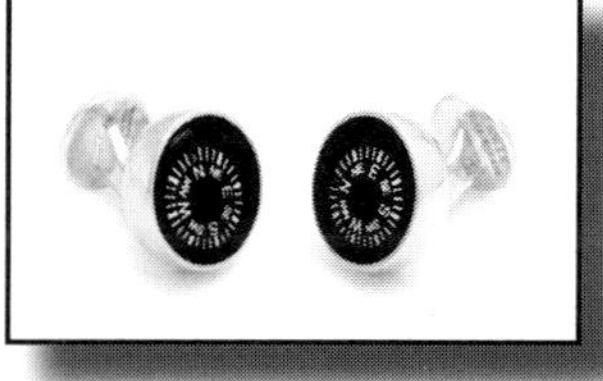

• Keep your loved ones close to home with playful compass jewelry. LeeAnn Herreid has designed these fun and functional accessories using sterling silver and real working compasses. Especially handy for the man who "never gets lost," these gifts are perfect for the directionally challenged and navigationally astute alike. You can order handmade compass rings, necklaces, or cuff links. Engrave your gift or present it with a sweet sentiment, for example, "So you can always find your way back to me." $56-$90. www.uncommongoods.com (Click on jewelry.)

• A wrist or pocket watch with an inscription, here are some ideas:

"I'll always have time for you"
"Forever in time with you"
"You make time fly"
"You make time stand still"
"There is no one else I would rather spend time with than you"

• A ring, gem, or jewel, maybe even a single loose stone to up-size the wedding ring stone you or she always secretly desired.

• Create your own love coupons such as "A chore of your choice day" or a gift certificate for a day of beauty at a spa. (See sample vouchers at the end of this book for more ideas.)

• Make a personalized CD filled with all of your favorite songs or a home video.

• Plant little chocolate hugs and kisses or a favorite candy for him/her to find. Old fashioned candy from the 50s, 60s, 70s or 80s... is still available after all these years.
www.oldtimecandy.com

• A locket with a photo in it to keep the one he/she loves close to his/her heart is a lovely gift. You can also put a lock of your hair in it.

• Lottery tickets

• Car wash tokens

• A good cigar, you can order one from: www.littlecigarfactory.com

• Tokens to redeem for a bucket of golf balls at a driving range

• Airline tickets to your favorite paradise or a photo of that "some day" fantasy vacation site. Include one action that you are committed to taking each week/month to turn this vacation fantasy into a reality.

• My gift selection: I asked a friend who lives in Las Vegas to mail me some "Treasure Island" slot machine coins. I planted these "treasure coins" inside of colored plastic Easter style eggs and hid them around the house. The last and largest plastic egg was a golden egg and it contained two tickets to Las Vegas in celebration of a birthday.

You don't have to be as outlandish as I am, but be creative and thoughtful with your hidden treasure to make it meaningful and memorable for your partner. Plant these little treasures inside of plastic Easter eggs, pepper them around the house and send your special person on the hunt!

Begin your evening by inviting your lover to this special event:

For the One I Love

"This evening of surprises begins with the reading of a treasure map and its story. You will be seated for a unique, yet informal dinner where the only way to nourish ourselves will be from each other's hands."

Travel to your enchanted island room for your meal. This meal is outstanding and so much fun! (Hands down and bar none, this is my favorite idea in the book!)

Bogan Island Treasure Hunt Dinner:

Read this entire section including the treasure map so you are familiar with all the steps that you will need to take during the course of this meal. This meal is to be eaten on the floor and is also to be eaten only with your hands. Place a sheet on the floor and then a foiled piece of cardboard on which the meal will be served. Set up an array of plush pillows for added comfort or simply sit "Indian style" on the floor. This atmosphere for your enchanted island feast is greatly enhanced by tons of candles and tea-lights; if possible turn off all of your electric lights and let the candles be the fire and the stars that would give you light outside on an island.

Tips before you get started:

Ask your partner to dress casually, but don't tell him/her anything about the evening he/she is about to experience. Let it be a surprise.

Don't let your partner see you set up the floor. Blindfold him/her or send him/her into another room until you are ready to lead him/her to the enchanted island.

Just before leading your partner onto the island, ask him/her to remove any jewelry (rings, bracelets, and watches) from his/her hands and wrists.

Refresh beverages prior to entering the room in which you will eat.

Ingredients for Bogan Island Treasure Hunt Dinner:

Yield: 2-4 (Dinner for two? Leftovers are equally tasty the second time around! Or, if you have petite appetites simply half this recipe)

1 box of moist towelettes

1 lb. boneless skinless chicken breast (substitutions beef tips or tofu)

1 can tomato soup (10 3/4 oz.)

1 can chicken broth (10 3/4 oz.)

1 can water (10 3/4 oz.)

1/2 large diced onion

1/2 tablespoon Lawry's seasoned salt

1/2 tablespoon curry powder 1/2 teaspoon garlic salt

4 oz can of mushrooms

1 can of green beans (14.5 oz. drain and cut into bite size pieces)

1 box of Uncle Ben's rice (not Minute Rice)

1/2 jar of mild salsa (12 oz. jar)

1/3 jar of hot salsa (12 oz. jar)

1 cup sliced almonds (toasted for flavor) or substitute 1 cup raisins

1 lemon (cut in quarters)

1 lime (cut in quarters)

1 small container sour cream

Directions:

Clean and cut chicken into cubes or strips and place raw into Dutch oven.

Then add the following ingredients:

1 can of tomato soup

1/2 can chicken broth

1/2 can water

1/2 large diced onion

1/2 tablespoon Lawry's seasoned salt

1/2 tablespoon curry powder

1/2 teaspoon garlic salt or 1-2 chopped garlic cloves.

Bring this mixture to a boil, then reduce heat and simmer for 20-30 minutes.

Remove the cooked chicken from the Dutch oven and set it aside on a lined cookie sheet. Sprinkle more Lawry's salt and curry powder on the chicken pieces, then bake at 350 degrees for about 12-15 minutes or until brown. The chicken may dry out fast, so check it often. When the chicken is done, just let it rest atop the stove on the cookie sheet. It is okay if it cools off before the rice is finished. Just leave the chicken alone.

In the Dutch oven, add the 4 oz can of mushrooms and the drained and cut green beans to the remaining broth mixture that you cooked the chicken in. Bring the mixture back to a boil. Once the broth is boiling, add 1 to 1 1/4 cup Uncle Ben's rice to mixture and reduce the heat to simmer for 20 min. (Minute Rice does not work.) Use your judgment on how much soup base is in the Dutch oven to determine how much rice to add. While stirring the rice, if you notice that it is dry, add some water or a little leftover chicken broth.

Keep stirring the rice so it doesn't stick. When the rice is done, the final product should be thick like stew, not soupy.

Feel free to liven up your foiled cardboard table with bread or biscuits and garden fresh tomatoes.

When you are ready to serve your dinner, follow steps #1-9 of the treasure map in sequence. Don't forget to have a box of moist towelettes available!

Photocopy or print the next page separately and fill in the blanks to personalize the story. Begin reading the lost treasure map of Bogan Island! Retrieve your free print ready PDF file of the map at: www.operationromance/treasurehunt/thankyou.html

Author's Note: Peach/Apple Crisp is a great dessert following this meal. Don't forget, you have to eat with your hands!

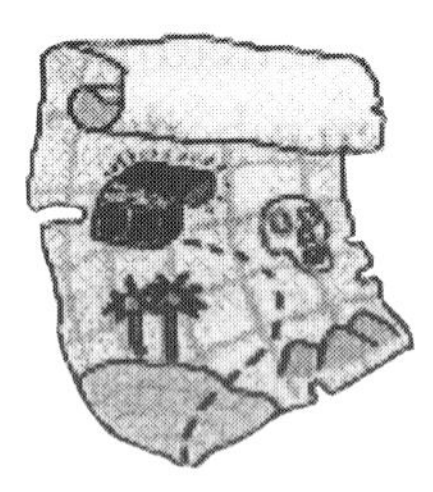

Treasure Map

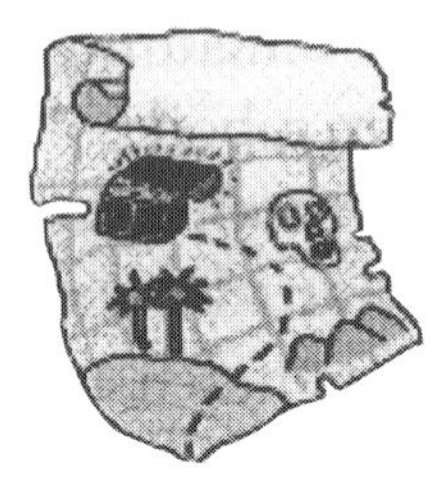

Vacation is finally here, and we are off to ___________ beach. It is a 90 degree day with a scorching sun, so we decide to go for a boat ride. We are certainly enjoying our day's festivities when suddenly the wind picks up and the sky turns black as night. The thunder and lightning come quickly, and we try to get back to the land, but the waves keep crashing against us and push us out to sea. Our boat sinks! We float on pieces of the wreckage for countless days. Finally, we land on a deserted shore. We drag our tired, sunburned, and weary selves up the beach and head directly to the palm trees that will shade us from the very hot sun. We lay there for hours dreaming of food and drinks, but are far too exhausted to try to look for some.

Finally, ____________ (your name) awakes and says, "We must find food and shelter and get our strength back so that we can be rescued." _________ (lover's name) says, "Let me come with you in case you need help carrying things." On our search, we are able to find some food and a few other useful items; we even drag dead, broken branches, and twigs behind us for firewood and shelter. From the corner of (his/her) eye ________ (lover's name) notices something washed ashore; it is someone's backpack. (He/She) quickly and vigorously rummages through it and is able to salvage a lighter! With that,____________ (your name) starts a fire to get the food going while____________(lover's name) rummages through the backpack again and sees, among a number of other items, a box of handy wipes.

Step 1: Pass the moist towelettes around at this time for both of you to wipe your hands thoroughly! And light all the candles.

____________ (lover's name) then hollers and points as (he/she) runs towards a cooler that must have survived the storm and washed up on the shore. Luck is on our side, there is ____________ (beer/soda/wine/rum) in it. We happily and well deservedly indulge!

Step 2: Pass out the beverage that each of you will be drinking with dinner.

However, we can't set the beverages on the ground for fear the Island bugs will crawl in them so ________ (lover's name) suggests that we each hold the beverage in our left hands for the remainder of the feast.

Step 3: You must not remove your beverage from your left hand for the entire meal!

In the search for food ______________ (lover's name) is also able to find a small patch of wild rice and secretly stuffs (his/her) pockets with it as a surprise.

Step 4: At this time, go and get the rice mixture and spread it onto the tin foil on the floor.

______________ (your name), with (his/her) rock throwing skills, is able to catch a wild bird as the main course for the feast.

Step 5: At this time, plop the chicken pieces onto the bed of rice.

The wind picks up again and a coconut falls from the palm tree and lands perfectly on a stone, breaking the coconut open and oozing its fresh, creamy nectar on top of the feast.

Step 6: Dab sour cream and sprinkle browned almonds on top of the feast.

The great wind blows yet again, and wouldn't you know it, some deep red berries come tumbling down too, so smash them up and use them for spices. With all the good luck we are having, we are certain to be rescued.

Step 7: Add dabs of the mixed salsa to top off the unique feast.

At last, we are ready to partake of this well deserved and hard earned meal, when all of the sudden________ (lover's name) realizes we have no utensils and since our left hands are already holding beverages, (he/she) suggests the only way to nourish ourselves is by our lover's hand. We are so hungry, nearly starving, so we do not speak a word throughout the whole meal! The wind continues to blow and blow and blow; out of nowhere lemons and limes come crashing down out of their resting places in the trees.

Step 8: At this time, pass the bowl of lemons and limes and ask your honey to squeeze the juice over the top of the feast.

Step 9: With right hands only, mix the food together. At this time, each of you must be holding your beverage in your left hand and only mixing and scooping up food with your right hand. Place that nourishment only in the mouth of your partner with your hand. From THIS point forward, no words are to be spoken for the remainder of the meal. One bite for him/ her...one bite for you! After the meal, only you (the

host) may speak as you continue reading the map to your partner and send him or her off on the treasure hunt. After an instruction, try to refrain from verbal communication. This is really an exercise about non-verbal communication and intimacy.

After you have nourished each other's body, continue reading the treasure map.

The sun is just beginning to set, so after the feast, we rush to build a shelter; still exhausted from surviving the vicious storm, we fall fast asleep. Suddenly, we are woken up by a hearty chuckle and a light poke of a sword to ______________'s (your name) throat. We were sleeping so deeply we didn't hear the pirate ship crash to the shore! "Get up, mate!" the pirate cries. "I says geet up!" with his sword still poking______________'s (your name) throat. He shouts to______________(lover's name), "You stays rights where you are," as he boasts a hearty chuckle. ______________(your name) cries out and pleads with the pirate to please let you both go, but the pirate continues to tie (him/her) to a tree, puts a gag in (his/her) mouth and a blindfold over (his/her) eyes. The pirate turns his sword to face ______________ (lover's name) and says, "You's commin with me." They vanish.

After hours and hours______________(your name) breaks free. (He/She) is careful not to be seen and recaptured or killed by the pirate. (He/She) wanders all over the island, hiding behind trees and bushes while searching for (his/her) lover. (He/She) searches and searches and searches, but to no avail. Finally and desperately, (he/she) thinks to leave______________(lover's name) some clues, dropping things that only (his/her) lover would recognize as significant. (He/She) scours the whole island dropping items along the way so ________ (lover's name) would know that (he/she) is free and is searching for (him/her).

Step 10: At this time, embark on the Treasure Hunt. Present the Keepsake box with the first clue inside it and start the treasure hunt. Once all of the treasure has been found, finish the story.

Suddenly,______________(your name) realizes that the pirate's ship is gone and that ______________ (lover's name) is probably on it. (He/She) becomes extremely depressed at the thought that (he/she) may never see ______________ (lover's name) again. ____________ (Your name) yearns to tell ______________ (lover's name) how much (he/she) loves (him/her). With tears in (his/her) eyes, ______________ (your name) sits down on the beach, looking out at the ocean, believing that ______________ (lover's name) is lost at sea with the pirate forever.

Desperately,______________(your name) runs into the crashing waves of the still wicked waters determined to swim after the ship, even if it means dying in the process.

(He/She) would rather die trying to find (his/her) love, than waste away on the beach. Instead of drowning, fate steps in and a current drags (him/her) away. Clinging to a piece of driftwood, (he/she) is again aimlessly drifting in the roaring sea. Hours later, (he/she) is thrown onto a strange shore by a giant wave. After being startled from the hard thrust of the water to the shore, (he/she) looks up and lo and behold there on the shoreline is the anchored pirate ship!

______________ (Your name) approaches the ship cautiously, but quickly, looking for any signs of the pirate and (his/her) beloved. (He/She) climbs up a rope on the side of the ship and slips aboard. (He/She) quietly approaches the main cabin and looks inside, and there, fast asleep, is the pirate! But there is no sign of ______________(lover's name) so (he/she) continues to search. Deep in the hold of the ship, (he/she) finds ______________ (lover's name) locked in a cell. (His/Her) lover points to the wall near the stairs and there hanging on a nail are the keys!______________(Your name) quickly grabs the keys, unlocks the cell and embraces ______________(lover's name). Silently, we climb the stairs to the ship's deck and just as we are about to escape, the pirate emerges from his cabin; spotting us. He grabs his sword and charges______________(your name). Just in a nick of time ______________ (your name) is able to jump aside as the pirate lunges with his sword and buries it deep into a barrel of whiskey. While the pirate struggles to free his blade, we both grab another barrel and knock the pirate overboard! We hoist the anchor together and the ship begins to leave the island and the pirate behind. ______________(your name) says to ______________ (your lover's name), "I never thought that I would see you again or have the chance to say how much I love you. I want to tell you every day from now on that I love you and am so glad that you are mine." After an embrace, they set sail heading toward the sunset, and live happily ever after.

The End.

Step 11: At this time, silently embrace your lover as if it is your last chance to. Tomorrow is promised to no one.

Tips for a story book ending: Personalize the end of the pirate story by saying whatever you have always wanted to say to your love. Be vulnerable and share your true feelings. For example:

- "I have loved you from the very first moment that I met you and I miss you every moment that I am not with you."
- "Please forgive me for being scared to show you the fire in my heart that burns for you; I was just too afraid that the feelings wouldn't be returned."

"Of all the wonders in all my travels, there is but one that leaves me eternally awed... seeing the joy of friends breaking bread –using their last loaf."

–Sgt. Traci

Special Bonus: Bogan Island Treasure Hunt Dinner For Friends

Sgt. Traci cooks her signature "Bogan Island" dinner for her friends and fellow authors, Mark S. A. Smith, Karyn Buxman and Greg Godek at Godek's home in LaJolla.

Bogan Island Treasure Hunt Dinner for Friends

Since this is such a fun, original, and unique dining experience, I believe it should also be shared with friends and not just between two people. I have decided to include some tips on how to revise the previous version so it can be shared with friends. If there is a special occasion for someone in the crowd, make that person feel special by making him or her, the "hero" of the story.

Tips for your Dinner Party:

6-8 guests are ideal for this dining experience.

The dinner runs more smoothly if there are two designated people helping, one meal presenter and one treasure map reader to coincide with the feast presentation.

- Tell your guests to dress casually. Tell them nothing about the evening they are about to experience. Let them be surprised.
- Don't let them see you set up the floor; I let my guests mingle in one room while I sneak off and set up our enchanted island in another.
- Just before leading your guests to Bogan Island, request that they remove all rings, bracelets, watches, and shoes.
- Request that they form a single file line and refresh their dinner drinks giving them just enough time to wonder what is going on and then lead them to their dining oasis.
- Really throw your guests for a loop! Send your guests an invitation for a formal dinner party...and then spring the Bogan Island Dinner on them! I did this once and it was that much more fun!
- I give each of my guests a small gift for the treasure hunt. I write their names on the plastic Easter eggs and hide them in one designated room. I ask that while they are hunting if they come across someone else's egg, to just leave it behind for the intended person to find.
- I stuff their eggs with fun, but inexpensive, little things like lottery tickets or scratch off tickets, a free drink token from their favorite

watering hole, car wash tokens or a token for a bucket of balls to a driving range, or an array of items from the Dollar Store. This is just a little something for them to take home and remember the evening by.

This truly is an outstanding tasting meal and is guaranteed to leave your friends talking about your unique dinner party! I bet they will ask for the recipe and instructions!

Begin by doubling the ingredients needed for the Bogan Island Dinner. Follow the recipes instructions with the added ingredients, ask your guests to hold their drinks in their left hands and eat only with their right hands. And of course, in this version, you get to laugh and talk all you want.

Photocopy or print out the Treasure Map pages for the dinner portion of the evening and fill in the blanks so you can better personalize the story by adding names that pertain to you and your guests. Get your free downloadable Treasure Map PDF at:
www.operationromance/treasurehunt/thankyou.html

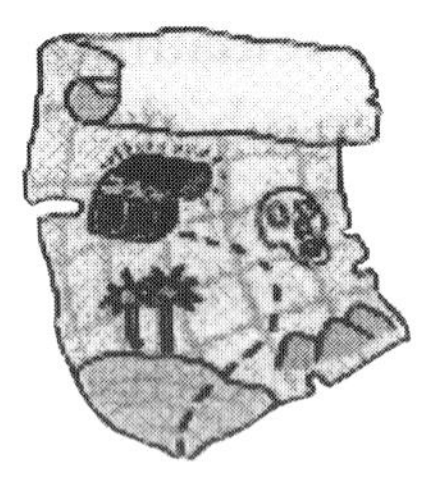

Treasure Map

The sun is just beginning to set, so after the feast, we rush to build a shelter; still exhausted from surviving the vicious storm, we fall fast asleep. Suddenly we are awakened by a hearty chuckle and a light poke of a sword to ____________ (guest honoree's) throat. We were sleeping so deeply, we didn't hear the pirate ship crash to the shore! "Get up me lady/mate!" The pirate cries, "I says geet up!" with his sword still poking ____________ (guest honoree's) throat. He shouts to everyone else, "You stays rights where you are ~ cuz yer all cumins with me," as he boasts a hearty chuckle. We cry out and plead with the pirate to please let us go, but the pirate proceeds to tie ____________ (guest honoree) to a tree, put a gag in (his/her) mouth, and a blindfold over (his/her) eyes. The pirate then draws his sword and says, "Now yer all commin with me." They all vanish. After struggling for hours, ____________ (guest honoree) breaks free. (He/She) cautiously begins searching the island for (his/her) friends, being careful not to be seen. As ________ (guest honoree) searches, (he/she) thinks to leave (his/her) friends' clues, dropping things and items that they would recognize as significant, so they would know that (he/she) was free and was searching for them.

Step 10: At this time send your guests on their Treasure Hunt!

When they return, finish the story.

_______________(Guest honoree) continues walking and searching and finally reaches the other side of the island. (He/She) is thinking that this island is much bigger than (he/she) realized last night, when (he/she) sees an inlet from the sea and the pirate ship anchored near shore. Hope fills (his/her) heart and quickly (he/she) works (his/her) way down to the beach. Looking around (he/she) spots some driftwood at the water's edge. (He/She) makes a dash for the wood and pushs it into the sea, using it as cover, (he/she) swims out to the pirate ship, finds a rope and hauls (himself/herself) up onto the ship. _____________(Guest honoree) cautiously searches the ship and finds (his/her) friends tied up in the cabin. (He/She) quickly unties (his/her) friends and asks where the pirate is. No one knows. They all go out on the deck and see the pirates emerging from the jungle on the shore with their rowboats pulled up on the beach. Quickly everyone helps pull up the anchor and the ship sets sail into the sunset!

_______________ (Guest honoree) is our hero!

The End

Pirate story written by: Traci Bogan based and built on the story my grandparents would read to us each time they treated us to this unique feast. Our family friend, Leslie Mudge helped write the original version. And a special thanks to the Schonert family, for sharing this wonderful dining experience with my grandparents, many years ago.

Secrets to Luxurious Baths

“Romance is like a luxurious warm bath on a cold winter night.”

–Sgt. Traci

The Bath

A Bubble bath is a wonderful, inexpensive way to treat yourself, as supplies are easy to find and you can tailor your bath to your heart's content. I love baths and the following bath recipes I have included in this section are simply a collection from my own personal experimentations through the years. Keep in mind that my preferences may vary from yours; my selected scents, colors, and textures may not agree with or appeal to your senses. Feel free to customize these recipes to your own liking by adding or substituting other salts, essential oils, herbs or textures.

To save time, thoroughly mix all suggested liquids/oils from the bath recipe ingredients in advance and bottle until you are ready to use them. Add the pre-bottled liquid to the bath water and then add the dry ingredients from the bath recipe, at tub time. Although it takes a little more effort, I recommend that you pre-make all of your bath recipes by mixing all the solids together in one bowl, and in a separate bowl, mix together all of your liquids/oils and then slowly add it to solids/salts, stirring well to prevent any clumps from forming. You should let it sit for a couple of hours before jarring, to allow the scent to be thoroughly and uniformly absorbed.

Baths salts can harden in high humidity areas, to remedy this, simply add a couple of tablespoons of glycerin to the bath recipe. Another important tip that will help prevent hardening is to make sure that your bottles are thoroughly washed and dried a day in advance before bottling your bath recipe.

These handmade bath recipes also make great gifts! Simply fill decorative jars or sentimental corked bottles with your loved one's favorite scented bath ingredients and write the recipe and instructions for use on a fancy gift-card and attach it to the bottle with a beautiful ribbon or some raffia. To create a tight seal for packaging or transport, dip the cork in melted wax then put it into the bottle.

Keep in mind the scents you choose for your candles and your bubble bath ingredients create different effects. Different scents dispel certain moods transporting you into heavenly peace or are so unpleasantly strong that they can ruin the intended relaxing moment. You can literally choose from thousands of scents available. A few good choices are evening blue bell or primrose to promote trust, longevity, and commitment; gardenia to renew passion; and for an aphrodisiac effect, try jasmine, lavender, nutmeg, sandalwood, cinnamon, allspice, vanilla, or rose. Raw oatmeal and fruits also add nice textures. Bath salts and essential oils are found at most specialty shops or can easily be purchased online. www.peacefulmind.com

For all bath recipes, I suggest using a piece of nylon to catch particles that may otherwise slip down the drain.

Be sure to add each ingredient to the warm running water as you fill the bath tub, to assure a thorough mix.

All bath and evening suggestions are to be experienced at your own risk!

It is said by many medical professionals that quality bath salts and some essential oils ease stressed and achy muscles, tension, and sports injuries. The relaxing element of hotwater complements the effects of the salts and essential oils. Aromatic baths can provide relief from stress and anxiety and assist with muscle and joint pain. It also provides deep relaxation, promotes restfulness, draws out impurities in the skin, helps detoxify the body and is suggested to stimulate natural circulation for improved health. Aesthetically, the effect of salts and essential oils smooths, softens, restores, and renews skin.

If you are on a budget, you can substitute fresh slices of lemons, limes, or other fresh fruit for the essential oils, which creates a different visual and textural effect.

Tips on adding luxury to a bathing experience:

Place candles in the bathroom to create soft light. If the occasion is appropriate and your bathtub is large enough, once your lover is in the bath, you can place a few floating candles in the tub.

In the evenings, dim the lights and play soft and appropriately themed music in the background to set the stage for romance.

Always warm the towels and your love's robe and slippers in the dryer before the bath is over. (If you don't have a dryer, you can warm towels, robes and slippers by wrapping them around or placing them on a heating pad.) There is nothing worse than getting out of the tub or shower into a cold room; either turn up the heat a notch or bring a small space heater into the bathroom. When your sweetie steps out of the bath tub, you should be ready to wrap him/her in something warm and soft.

Keep your favorite beverage chilled in a nearby ice bucket. Serve with chilled glasses that were pre-stowed in the freezer. Start your bath off with a toast for two, or better yet, enjoy a "double-bubble" and bathe together.

Engrave a special message into a new and nicely scented bar of soap with a toothpick and leave for your sweetheart to find or write on the shower walls with kids' bath crayons, this works surprisingly well.

Fill little plastic Easter eggs or the little plastic balls from a gum ball machine with fortune cookie sized laminated suggestive and daring notes and float them in the tub.

Write a love note, special message, or invitation with lipstick or soap onto the bathroom mirror, so it is the first thing that your significant other sees in the morning.

Plushy oversized bath towels, terry-cloth bathrobes, fuzzy slippers, and fresh silk or satin sheets on the bed are always a nice added touch. Having them monogrammed is really impressive.

If your bar of soap keeps slipping from your hands and getting lost at the bottom of the tub while you are bathing your partner, try Ivory soap. It actually floats!

To prepare for the bath, slowly disrobe/undress your partner, working your way from the top down. You may suggestively lead him/her to sit on the tub's edge or the closed toilet seat as you peel away the rest of his/her clothing. As he/she rests for a moment, be sure to test the bath water's temperature, get his/her approval by letting a few beaded droplets melt onto his/her inner wrist.

Try ending an evening's bath with a short, but ever so sweet, foot rub. Gently brush the feet using circular motions with a soft body brush or your hands, starting at the feet and work your way up the calves. This light brushing technique removes dead skin cells while stimulating circulation, and it feels good!

You can also add to the tub service with a gentle and intimate shampoo and scalp massage. Kneel on a towel for your comfort, and with your cupped hands, begin to warm your partner's non submerged body parts with handfuls of velvety water. Using the same method, wet his/her hair. Apply shampoo to the base of your palm and spread it evenly in your hands and begin the shampooing process. Start at the top of the head by the forehead and work your way down the scalp towards the nape of the neck in total and complete silence. Give a gentle scalp massage and lather well, using circular motions. Place the very tips of your fingers on the temples and apply gentle pressure in a slow circular motion. With gentle pressure trace your fingers back behind the ears and to the neck at base of the skull. Continue rubbing the neck and shoulders to complete the relaxation. Cover his/her eyes with a washcloth and gently rinse. Give at least a 3-5 minute hair wash and scalp massage.

Another intimate way to enhance a bath is to offer a shave of his/her choice.

A full body wash is another way to add intimacy to a luxury bath. You can use your bare hands, a mitt, wash cloth, or a bath sponge, depending on what you are most comfortable with. (The following instructions are written for bare hands.)

• Start with the face, using both your index and middle finger of one hand, lightly soap your two fingers (don't directly soap the face) then tenderly trace the contours and features. Continue the same soft, gentle circular motions beginning with the forehead and working your way around your partner's face in a clockwise fashion, excluding the eyes. You will need to re-soap your two fingers upon every quarter. Then carefully rinse.

• Next move down to the neck, lightly soap your hands, this time use the finger tips of both hands and execute slow circular massage style motions to the back base of the neck, while securing your thumbs lightly onto the outer chin region for support. Use your pinky fingers to catch behind the ears and again to the inner base of the ears. Switch to one hand, still using your finger tips, upon reaching the front of the neck. Gently rinse.

• When soaping the chest and stomach area, place one hand behind the upper back and use your other full palm to apply a circular and lightly pressured massage. Keep an even rhythm, pressure and pace. Use your pinky finger or a cotton swab to soap the belly button. Lift his/ her arms out of the water one at a time and work from the shoulder down to the wrist. Use one of your hands to hold the arm up and the other of your hands to soap it. Use a gentle figure eight style motion, this will allow you to catch his/her back and forearm at the virtually the same time. When you get to the hands, interlock your fingers with your lovers and use your thumb to gently wash and massage the palm. Use your thumb and forefinger to bathe the fingers. Repeat on other side.

• If you and your sweetie are comfortable with bathing the genital region, the best way to thoroughly reach this area, is with a simple position transfer to all fours. Respect his/her vulnerability. In a completely non-sexual manner, soap the bottom and genitalia using gentle circular motions, and then have him/her sit back for an automatic rinse. Remember to always apply the soap to your hands and not to the body directly. If either of you are not comfortable with this, simply skip to the next step. Your partner will have a chance to do it him/ herself at bath's end.

• Continue down to the thighs and legs. Washing one leg at a time, use both full hands, one on either side of the leg, to execute the same gentle circular massage style techniques as above. Begin at the upper thigh of one leg work your way down to the foot and repeat to the other leg. Pay meticulous attention to the sweet spots around the knee caps, behind the knees, on the ankles, feet and between the toes. I prefer to use a single soapy thumb with that same lightly pressured circular motion for these areas in particular. Allow at least 30-60 seconds per region. Use your thumb on the feet with the same gentle circular motions and if your partner has stubby little toes, you can use a soapy cotton swab to clean between them.

• Spend around 3-5 minutes on the hair wash and foot bath portion. If you have one, a removable shower head offers a more thorough, up close and personal body rinse.

• Now that you know your sweetie has clean feet, you may consider softly sucking the toes or gently kissing and caressing the feet with your lips. Or a simple velvet kiss to the brow is a sweet gesture. Remember, silence is golden.

Morning Delight Bubble Bath

For this bath, invite your loved one to something like this:

Wake up in a foamy bubble bath scented to stimulate your senses and help you start your day off right.

Directions:

Fill tub with water drawn at a comfortable temperature

Add 1 cup of pre-made recipe mix or add 1 cup of sea-salt, Epsom salt, or a ½ cup of each, or 1 cup of powdered milk

Add 8 drops of Comfrey (Comfrey produces an exhilarating bath for when you want to feel wide-awake.)

Add 5 drops of yellow food coloring to water

Add 3 count pour of his or her favorite foamy bubble bath

Substitute:

If you do not have Comfrey, orange, and ginger are also wonderful aromas that stimulate and wake the senses. Try grating ginger and orange peel into the water and then slicing the orange and floating the pieces in the bath.

Especially for this Bath:

Offer your sweetheart his/her favorite morning beverage to sip on while he/she wakes up in this bath. A mug of coffee or tea, a glass of juice or a yogurt smoothie would all work well.

Float a rubber duck in the water for a playful morning.

Offer your love a gentle loofah massage to stimulate and refresh the skin before starting the day.

Roman Times Leisure Bath

For this bath, invite your loved one to something like this:

Pamper yourself in this inviting restoration bubble bath that is abundant with luscious aromas, rejuvenation potions, and fresh daisies.

Directions:

Fill tub with water drawn at a comfortable temperature

Add 1 cup of pre-made recipe mix or add 1 cup of sea-salt, Epsom salt, or a 1/2 cup of each, or 1 cup of powdered milk

Add 1/4 cup of any fine quality natural oil (the Romans were thought to have used olive or sesame oil)

Add 1 tsp. of baking powder

Add 5 drops lime scented oil or juice

Add 4 drops fig oil

Add 5 drops green food coloring to water

Add 3 count pour of foamy bubble bath, mild baby shampoo, or Castile liquid soap

Substitute:

If preparing this bath takes too much time or costs too much, simply fill the tub with water, add a few drops of green food coloring, then some bubbles and/or bath salt, and if available, a few fresh daisy heads.

Especially for this Bath:

Lead your loved one to the bath and help him/her in, while he/she drifts back to Roman times, retrieve a prepared platter of grapes, cheese, fig cookies, and a glass of sparkling wine. Serve him/her as if he/she were a god/goddess and you were his/her personal slave.

By the glow of the candlelight, softly recite a classic poem or a love-letter you wrote for your sweetie. For a large assortment of classic love poems, visit: www.theromantic.com. Or use my personal favorite, How do I love thee? by Elizabeth Barrett Browning, which is listed on the following page.

When your sweetie is ready to face the 21st century again, retrieve freshly warmed towels, bathrobe and slippers, pat your partner dry and help him/her robe.

How do I love thee? Sonnet 43

How do I love thee? Let me count the ways.
I love thee to the depth and breadth and height
My soul can reach, when feeling out of sight
For the ends of being and ideal Grace.
I love thee to the level of every day's
Most quiet need, by sun and candle-light.
I love thee freely, as men strive for Right;
I love thee purely, as they turn from Praise.
I love thee with the passion put to use
In my old grief's, and with my childhood's faith.
I love thee with a love I seemed to lose
With my lost saints,—I love thee with the breath,
Smiles, tears, of all my life!—and, if God choose,
I shall but love thee better after death.
--Elizabeth Barrett Browning

99 Candle Bubbling Rose Bath

For this bath, invite your loved one to something like this:

> *Enjoy this bath, where mountains of cloud-like bubbles are sprinkled with rose petals or freshly clipped rose blooms on top of the velvet colored water to send you deep into long lasting dreams.*

Directions:

Fill tub with water drawn at a comfortable temperature

Add 1 cup of your pre-made recipe mix or add 1 cup sea salt or Epsom salt or a 1/2 cup of each

Add 1/2 cup dry powdered milk

Add 5 drops rose scented oil

Add 5 drops vanilla scented oil

Add 3-5 drops of red food coloring to water

Add 3 count pour of favorite foamy bubble bath

Substitute:

If preparing this bath takes too much time or costs too much, simply fill the tub with water, add a few drops of red food coloring, then some bubbles and/or bath salt, and if you can, add a couple rose heads or rose petals atop.

Especially for this Bath:

Lace the bath water with rose petals and rose bud tips (cut off the stem or buy them already broken from a florist for around $5/bag)

You can sprinkle any extras on the floor, counter top, and in the toilet water. This looks beautiful!

Serve your partner with a platter of white/chocolate covered strawberries or other fruit and with champagne. Remember to put a single strawberry in the bottom of the champagne flute.

Golden Sunset Bath

For this bath, invite your loved one to something like this:

Come recline in the warm, foamy water as these soothing aromas calm your senses leading you to a state of blissful relaxation.

Directions:

Fill tub with water drawn at a comfortable temperature

Add 1 cup of your pre-made recipe mix or add 1cup of sea salt or Epsom salt or a 1/2 cup of each

Add 1 cup of powdered milk

Add 8 drops of your favorite scented or essential oil. (For this bath Chamomile, Mint and Lavender work beautifully since they are soothing and relaxing scents.)

Add 3-5 drops of his or her favorite color food coloring

Add a 3 count pour of his or her favorite foamy bubble bath

Add fresh wild flowers or mini sunflowers heads

Substitute:

If preparing this bath takes too much time or costs too much, simply fill the tub with water, add a few drops of his/her favorite color food dye, then some bubbles and/or bath salt, and place a few wild flower heads, plucked from your yard or the side of the road, on top.

Especially for this Bath:

Place a message in a bottle and float it in the tub. If you have one, use a bottle from a previous special occasion you shared together, inside slip a simple cut out heart bearing your initials, a love note, or a coupon, then cork it and float in underneath the bubbles.

Add small chunks of dry ice around the corners of the tub and in the bathroom sink; see how mesmerizing and seductive the fog is. Or strategically place it on the floor for a thin layer of a foggy, mystic feel. You could enhance this picturesque scene of foggy mist on the floor by using lit candles to form a pathway that shows the way to the tub. A small fogger machine is equally mystic and daring. Light your candles and turn off the lights.

Ease A Cold Bubble Bath

A great way to ease the symptoms from a common cold is to draw your partner this hot and relaxing "breathe easy" bubble bath.

For this bath, invite your loved one to something like this:

Come and relax in this soothing bath. Eucalyptus oil is known to ease cold congestion and Epsom salt is known to "draw-out" impurities and relieve aches and pains. I love you and hope that this bath will be the perfect remedy for your cold. Feel better soon!

Directions:

Fill tub with water drawn at a comfortable temperature

Add 8 drops of eucalyptus oil

Add 3 drops of spearmint oil

Add 3 drops of peppermint oil

Add 4 cups of Epsom salt

Add 1-4 oz. bar of castille soap (available at most essential oil or "bath" shops)

Substitute:

If you do not have the essential oils for this bath, you can substitute any clean and comforting smells, green tea, or peppermint tea would work well as an alternative.

Especially for this Bath:

Bring your sweetie a tall glass of water while they soak in this bath to help keep him/her hydrated and flushing the cold germs away.

Offer a gentle massage wherever they feel aches or pains.

After the bath bring a hot cup of tea with soothing honey and some fresh lemon juice in it for extra vitamin C.

Once your partner has been dried and dressed in comfortable clothes bring a warm heating pad or compress for their shoulders and neck. If he/she has a headache, offer to bring a cool towel or eye mask for their forehead.

Bath Adventure à la Carte

Create your own ideal bath experience: just mark your selection (s), and submit this form to your partner to redeem your romantic time together.

For the One I Love

__ *Snack Service*
__ *Beverage Service*
__ *Background Music*
__ *Candles*
__ *Bubbles*
__ *Essential Oils*
__ *Rose petals / Flowers*
__ *Warmed Towel*
__ *Warmed Bathrobe & Slippers*
__ *Modest, Tasteful Disrobing*
__ *Essential Nail Care*
__ *Gentle Shampoo & Conditioning*
__ *Scalp and Temple Massage*
__ *Careful & Close Shave Of Choice*
__ *Loofah Sponge Wash*
__ *Foot Massage*
__ *Relaxing Back / Neck Rub*
__ *Full Body Wash*
__ *Poetry / Story Telling*
__ *Pat Down Dry*
__ Tuck Into Bed

If you are interested in creating more of your own specialized bath recipes, the Essential Oils table on the next page will show you which oils are believed to relieve ailments, enhance or dispel moods, and generally please the senses. I hope that you will be creative with this information and thoroughly enjoy the results.

Whichever baths you choose or create on your own, use the time to treat your lover as if he/she is the only person on earth at that moment. Do everything to him/her that you yourself would like, dream, or wish to have done to you. Indulge your partner, spoil him/her, and treat him/her as if he/she were a prince or goddess. For this day in this moment, live only to please and serve your special person.

Essential Oils

**"If the flesh is but dust,
love is the water that
washes away the flesh
between two souls."**

–Sgt. Traci

Essentials Oils

Special thanks to our friends for the following contribution:
www.peacefulmind.com

To Ease:	Try:
Abrasions	Geranium
Abscesses	Lavender
Aches	Eucalyptus, Lavender, Lemongrass, Peppermint, and Rosemary
Acne	Bergamot, Cedarwood, Lavender, and Tea Tree
Acute Fear	Geranium, Ylang Ylang
Aging Skin	Geranium, Sweet Orange
Aggression	Bergamot, Cedarwood, Chamomile, Juniper, Lemon, Marjoram, Rosemary, Ylang Ylang
Analgesic	Bergamot, Cajeput, Eucalyptus, Geranium, Lavender, Rosemary
Anger	Chamomile, Lavender, Marjoram, Rosemary, Ylang Ylang,
Anti-bacterial	Bergamot, Eucalyptus, Lavender, Patchouli
Anti-cancer	Geranium
Anti-convulsive	Clary Sage
Anti-depressant	Allspice, Bergamot, Clary Sage, Geranium, Grapefruit, Lavender, Ylang Ylang
Anti-inflammatory	Bergamot, Cinnamon, Geranium, Lavender, Patchouli, Peppermint

Antiseptic	Bergamot, Cajeput, Cedarwood, Cinnamon, Clary Sage, Eucalyptus, Fir Needle, Geranium, Lavender, Lemon, Lemongrass, Patchouli, Rosemary, Sweet Fennel
Anti-spasmodic	Eucalyptus, Sweet Fennel
Anti-viral	Bergamot, Cajeput, Cinnamon, Eucalyptus
Anxiety	Bergamot, Cedarwood, Clary Sage, Geranium, Grapefruit, Orange, and Ylang Ylang
Aphrodisiac	Cedarwood, Cinnamon, Clove, Clary Sage, Patchouli, Sweet Fennel
Appeasing	Patchouli
Arousing	Ylang Ylang
Arteriosclerosis	Rosemary
Arthritis	Basil, Black pepper, Lemon, Eucalyptus, Ginger
Congestion	Eucalyptus, Lavender, Rosemary
Cooling	Eucalyptus, Peppermint, Spearmint
Coughs	Allspice, Lavender
Courage Booster	Basil
Cracked Skin	Lavender, Patchouli
Cramps	Allspice
Criticism	Grapefruit

Crying	Clary Sage
Curbs Appetite	Patchouli, Sweet Fennel
Cuts	Lavender
Cystitis	Eucalyptus
Dandruff	Cedarwood, Clary Sage, Tea Tree
Deodorizing	Anise, Basil, Cajeput, Cinnamon, Citronella, Clary Sage, Eucalyptus, Lemongrass, Lime
Dependency	Grapefruit
Depression	Bergamot, Clary Sage, Lime, Sweet Orange
Dermatitis	Bergamot, Geranium, Lavender
Detoxifying	Grapefruit, Lemon, Sweet Fennel
Digestive	Cedarwood
Discontentment	Geranium
Disinfecting	Fir Needle, Lemon, Rosemary, Ylang Ylang
Disorientation	Cajeput, Rosemary
Distrust	Lemon
Dry Skin	Geranium, Lavender, Sweet Orange
Eczema	Bergamot, Geranium, Lavender

Emphysema	Eucalyptus
Emptiness	Bergamot
Encourages Menstruation	Basil
Encourages Vivid Dreams	Clary Sage
Energizing	Anise, Cajeput, Cinnamon, Clove, Grapefruit, Lemon, Lemongrass, Rosemary, Spearmint, Sweet Fennel
Envy	Grapefruit
Equalizing	Lime
Erases Doubt	Basil
Erotic	Cinnamon, Jasmine, Patchouli, Rose, Vanilla, Ylang Ylang
Euphoric	Clary Sage, Ylang Ylang
Explosive Emotions	Eucalyptus
Fatigue	Allspice, Clove, Geranium, Grapefruit, Lemon, Peppermint, Rosemary, Sweet Orange
Fear of Failure	Sweet Fennel
Fevers	Eucalyptus, Lemon, Lemongrass
Flatulence (Gas)	Allspice, Lavender, Lemongrass
Flea Repellent	Patchouli
Flu	Citronella, Clove, Eucalyptus, Sweet Orange, Tea Tree

Forgetfulness	Basil, Cajeput, Peppermint, Rosemary
Frustration	Grapefruit, Ylang Ylang
Fungal Infections	Clove, Tea Tree
Gall Stones	Rosemary
Gout	Rosemary
Grief	Bergamot, Grapefruit
Guilt	Clary Sage, Ylang Ylang
Hangovers	Rosemary
Hardens Nails	Lemon
Harmonizing	Cedarwood, Fir Needle, Lavender
Head Lice	Lavender
Headache	Basil, Lavender, Lemongrass, Lime, Rosemary
Heartache	Geranium, Rose
Helplessness	Bergamot
Herpes Simplex	Eucalyptus, Lycine, Tea Tree
High Blood Pressure	Lavender, Ylang Ylang
High Cholesterol	Rosemary

Hopelessness	Bergamot, Sweet Orange
Hostility	Clary Sage
Hot Flashes	Grapefruit, Lavender
Hyperactivity	Lavender
Hysteria	Tea Tree
Increases Intuition	Lavender
Increases Alertness	Basil, Lemon, Rosemary
Increases Creativity	Rosemary
Increases Sensitivity	Rosemary
Indecisiveness	Basil, Patchouli, Rosemary
Indigestion	Allspice, Lemon, Peppermint, Rosemary, Spearmint, Sweet Fennel, Tangerine
Infections	Lavender, Sweet Orange, Tea Tree
Inflammation	Lavender
Insect Bites	Lavender, Tea Tree
Insect Repellent	Bergamot, Cajeput, Citronella, Eucalyptus, Lemongrass, Spearmint, Tea Tree
Insomnia	Bergamot, Lavender, Tangerine, Ylang Ylang
Intoxicating	Clary Sage

Invigorating	Basil, Eucalyptus, Rosemary, Wintergreen
Irrational Thinking	Eucalyptus, Lemon
Irritability	Ylang Ylang
Irritated Skin	Geranium
Itching	Lavender, Peppermint, Thyme
Jealousy	Grapefruit, Ylang Ylang
Muscle Cramps	Allspice
Muscle Spasms	Allspice
Nausea	Allspice, Ginger, Lavender, Lemon, Peppermint
Nervous Exhaustion	Allspice, Basil, Clary Sage, Geranium, Lemongrass, Patchouli, Spruce, Sweet Fennel
Nervousness	Bergamot, Clary Sage, Fir Needle, Tangerine
Neuralgia	Allspice, Citronella, Geranium, Peppermint
Normalizes Emotions	Bergamot, Geranium, Lavender, Sweet Fennel, Ylang Ylang
Obesity	Grapefruit
Obsession	Clary Sage
Oily Skin	Cedarwood, Citronella, Clary Sage, Geranium, Grapefruit, Lemon
Pain	Clary Sage, Eucalyptus, Geranium, Lavender, Lemongrass, Rosemary

Panic Attacks	Lavender
Phlegm	Eucalyptus
PMS	Clary Sage, Geranium, Grapefruit, Sweet Fennel
Pneumonia	Eucalyptus
Poor Circulation	Allspice, Eucalyptus, Grapefruit, Lemongrass, Rosemary
Post Natal Depression	Clary Sage
Premature Balding	Rosemary
Prevents Sleep	Patchouli
Problem Skin	Lavender, Tea Tree
Psoriases	Bergamot, Geranium, Lavender
Rashes	Lavender
Refines Pores	Spearmint
Refreshing	Basil, Bergamot, Cinnamon, Fir Needle, Grapefruit, Lavender, Lemon, Lemongrass, Lime, Spearmint, Wintergreen
Rejuvenating	Geranium, Grapefruit, Lemon, Rosemary
Relaxing	Anise, Bergamot, Cajeput, Clove, Clary Sage, Geranium, Lavender, Lemongrass, Spearmint, Sweet Fennel
Resisting Change	Sweet Fennel

Respiratory Problems	Cedarwood, Eucalyptus, Fir Needle, Peppermint, Spruce
Restlessness	Clary Sage
Restoring	Geranium, Rosemary, Sweet Fennel
Rheumatism	Allspice, Citronella, Lavender, Sweet Fennel
Ringworm	Tea Tree
Romantic	Clary Sage, Patchouli
Scrapes	Lavender
Sedative	Bergamot, Cedarwood, Clary Sage, Geranium, Lavender, Lemongrass
Self Absorption	Ylang Ylang
Sense Enhancing	Allspice, Anise, Geranium
Sensual	Clary Sage, Patchouli, Ylang Ylang
Shingles	Eucalyptus
Shock	Peppermint, Tea Tree
Sinusitis	Basil, Eucalyptus, Lavender
Skin Conditioning	Bergamot, Cinnamon, Citronella, Clary Sage, Eucalyptus, Grapefruit, Lemongrass, Lime, Spearmint
Skin Spots	Cajeput
Soothing	Basil, Bergamot, Cajeput, Citronella, Clove, Clary Sage, Eucalyptus, Geranium, Grapefruit, Lavender, Lemongrass, Lime, Patchouli, Spearmint

Sore Muscles	Allspice, Basil, Citronella, Eucalyptus
Sore Throat	Lavender, Tea Tree
Sores	Patchouli
Sorrow	Eucalyptus
Sprains	Lavender
Stabilizing	Geranium
Stiffness	Allspice, Geranium
Stimulates Memory	Basil
Stimulating	Cajeput, Cinnamon, Clove, Eucalyptus, Grapefruit, Lavender, Lemongrass, Peppermint, Rosemary, Spearmint
Stings	Tea Tree
Stomach Disorders	Sweet Fennel, Sweet Orange
Strengthening	Basil, Cedarwood, Lavender, Lemon, Rosemary
Strengthens Immune System	Cajeput, Sweet Orange, Tea Tree
Stress	Allspice, Basil, Bergamot, Cedarwood, Clary Sage, Geranium, Grapefruit, Lavender, Lemongrass, Lime, Patchouli, Spruce, Sweet Fennel, Sweet Orange, Ylang Ylang
Stretch marks	Tangerine
Sunburn	Eucalyptus, Lavender

Tension	Allspice, Clary Sage, Geranium, Rosemary, Sweet Fennel, Sweet Orange, Ylang Ylang
Tightening	Grapefruit
Tonifying	Anise, Basil, Clary Sage, Eucalyptus, Grapefruit, Patchouli, Rosemary, Sweet Fennel
Tranquilizing	Geranium
Ulcers	Geranium
Uplifting	Anise, Bergamot, Clary Sage, Geranium, Grapefruit, Lemon, Patchouli, Rosemary, Ylang Ylang
Uterine Hemorrhage	Geranium
Vaginal Infection	Eucalyptus
Viral Infection	Tea Tree
Vitalizing	Cinnamon, Spearmint
Warming	Allspice, Anise, Cinnamon, Citronella, Clary Sage, Geranium, Rosemary
Warts	Lemon, Tea Tree
Water Retention	Geranium, Lavender, Patchouli, Rosemary
Whooping Cough	Sweet Fennel
Worry	Clary Sage, Lemon
Wounds	Eucalyptus, Lavender, Tea Tree
Wrinkles	Clary Sage

Please consult with a physician, naturopathic, homeopathic specialist, or shaman healer before using any essential oil. Please note that pure essential oils are highly concentrated substances and should be used with care and caution. Take the time to familiarize yourself with the use and application procedures of each individual oil that you are intending to use. Never take essential oils internally! Do not apply undiluted essential oils directly on the skin. The recommended Aromatherapy standard dilution is: 1-3%, though certain oils may be used in higher or lower dilutions depending on the individual oil. Always follow the recommended dilutions and quantities of each product. Keep your oils out of reach of children and pets. Sensitive skin types are advised to test oils on a small area of the inner arm prior to use. Avoid eye contact. Many oils should not be used during pregnancy. If pregnant, consult with your doctor and an aroma-therapist for suitability and safety of specific oils. If you suffer from a serious medical condition such as (but not exclusively) high blood pressure, cancer, thrombosis, varicose veins, or epilepsy consult your doctor, and a qualified aroma-therapist or other specialist for professional advice on recommended oils and doses. You can also research any essential oil at the National Association for Holistic Aromatherapy:
www.naha.org

Top Secret:

Chef Tory Miller's Recipes for Romance

"Romance is the spice that satisfies a woman's heart, appreciation is the herb that fortifies her soul."

–Sgt. Traci

Food is incredibly sensual and romantic. Everything about food is designed to appeal to the senses. It is remarkable that both men and women feel pampered, loved, and doted on when they are cared for through food. Whether you cook food for them, take them out to eat, or simply arrange for take-out and present it well at home, addressing this basic human need in creative ways communicates volumes to your loved one and adds a dash of romance to a daily necessity.

The love of delicious food has always been central to Chef Tory's culinary philosophy. At L'Etoile, the love begins with ingredients that were carefully cultivated by our farmers. The ingredients are then hand-selected at the farmers market by Chef Tory and L'Etoile's foragers. Finally, they are prepared by our chefs for our guests with patience, care, and a nuanced understanding of the blending of flavors and textures. The meal is then served with grace and finesse, in a comfortable ambience where all of the details are noted - the music, lighting, flowers, and candles have all been attended to. The end result is a meal that pleases each of the guest's senses ... sight, sound, smell, taste, and touch.

Food lovers often travel great distances and go to great lengths to enjoy meals prepared and served with this level of care and attention to detail. Whether you and your significant other consider yourselves food lovers or not, there is a great deal of love and romance that can be achieved in carefully preparing to nourish each other with food. This section of the book is meant to inspire you to creatively develop meals that will please the senses and evoke feelings of well-being and comfort in your significant other. It is fun to prepare something for another to enjoy, and it is fun to work together to prepare a favorite meal. It is important to note that the more time you and your loved one spend together, the more opportunities you will have to be romantic. Try working together on a meal at least once a week and enjoy the benefits of the added time to talk to each other, to be a team working towards a common goal, and the delicious food that results. Hopefully, these recipes will inspire you to be romantic whether you are teaming up in the kitchen or surprising one another.

Naturally, I encourage you to find more recipes and options to satisfy your individual tastes and desires. There are so many wonderful recipes out there. You should look around to find recipes that challenge you, but are not daunting. You will also get much more comfortable as you go along!

One of my favorite Web site recipe collections:

This site offers just about every type of recipe imaginable in a variety of categories for cooking and cooking-related information. It is loaded with recipes to accommodate every meal, party, and festive occasion from holiday and seasonal cooking, to ethnic dishes, health food options, and desserts. You can brush up on your etiquette, learn how to use your kitchen equipment, browse through or order vintage cookbooks, and get a crash course on the best wine producers. They also provide fantastic charts to help you develop your knowledge of metric equivalents, herbs and spices and a dictionary of wine and cooking terms. www.epicurious.com

The Ingredients are Important

Although everyone has different personal tastes when it comes to food, it is always true that fresh food tastes the best. Although it is not always feasible to use organic and locally grown food, when you want to prepare a stellar meal for someone, the best place to start is with the best ingredients. Here in Madison, Wisconsin, we are extremely fortunate. L'Etoile is located on the Capitol Square, which is also home to one of the largest farmers markets in the country. The locally grown, grass-fed meats, the artisan cheeses, and the fresh produce we have available here are all stellar. Although these ingredients may not be as easy to come by where you live, if you take the time to seek out quality ingredients like these in your area, your meals will definitely benefit from the added flavor and fantastic fresh textures. You will also find that you are eating healthier foods that are richer in vitamins and minerals, supporting your local economy and local farmers, and are contributing to a more sustainable society for future generations. The reasons to pay attention to what you eat and where it comes from are so numerous it is no wonder that more and more people are reading labels and asking questions about the food they purchase. We hope you will join them and start enjoying these benefits soon, if you aren't already!

This website offeres a full national listing of farmers markets by state: www.ams.usda.gov/farmersmarkets/map.htm

If you do not find a farmers market nearby, ask at your local grocery store if they have a section that features locally grown or organic produce. If they don't yet, they might consider starting one if more customers inquire about it.

Basic Preparation Tips:

Once you know what you want to prepare, you should take a few moments to make a plan to execute the meal.

First, read through all of your recipes. It is important to know if you need any special equipment, how long the recipes will take, and what steps are involved. Taking a moment to coordinate when you turn on one pot and when a dish gets placed in the oven, helps you avoid a headache when you are in the middle of cooking your dinner.

Make a list of all of the ingredients you need. You do not want to be elbow-deep in dough when you realize that you are out of flour! It is wise to check your fridge and your cupboards before you start cooking or baking and make a quick trip to the grocery store or your local farmers market if you need to.

Whenever possible, get all of your washing, chopping, and measuring done before you start cooking. That way you can keep your attention on the pots that need stirring and on what is happening with your ingredients … you will be much less likely to burn a dish if you aren't overly distracted.

Presentation is also Important

Even if you are serving a simple meal to your sweetheart, the act of plating the food and presenting it demonstrates effort and care in a powerful way. There are many ways to garnish a plate; here are just a few suggestions:

- Fresh herbs add color, fragrance, and panache to a plate. Try placing a sprig of parsley, rosemary, mint, or basil on a plate.

Try to match the herb to the flavors you were cooking with, although parsley is a great default for savory food and mint is a perfect default for dessert plates.

• Chopped herbs look beautiful when dusted on top of food or when sprinkled lightly around the perimeter of a plate. Dust or sprinkle powdered sugar for desserts.

• Drizzling extra sauce on top of a dish or on the plate of a dish makes everything more elegant. Drizzle sauce on the plate in any pattern and then set your food on top of it for a different effect.

• Garnishes can also be made by thinly slicing fruits and vegetables to accent the corner of a plate. Adding color to the presentation enhances the beauty of the food, so any colorful fruit or vegetable will work well.

Playing with your Food

Here are some fun and cute ideas to enhance your everyday romantic experiences with food. Try a few and see if they don't make you smile.

• Make heart shaped ice cubes and serve them in a favorite cold beverage on a hot summer day.

Simply buy a heart shaped tin from your local craft/hobby shop, fill with water or juice, and freeze. Try adding a single piece of fruit in each cube, like a slice of a strawberry and a splash of strawberry juice mixed with the water, before freezing.

• Show up at your partner's place of employment with a box of croissants, bagels, muffins, or doughnuts to share and enjoy with colleagues. Order Chinese or pizza on your credit card and have it delivered to your partner's work with a special message or a fortune cookie attached. Purchase a large enough spread to make sure your partner is able to share with peers.

• If your partner is normally the cook, give him or her the night off and cook the meal yourself. If you want to be silly and play up the fact that your partner is a chef, eat your soup with large measuring spoons, drink your beverages from measuring cups, and use neatly arranged aprons as your place setting or table cloth. Present him or her with a small gift - a personalized embroidered apron or a set of engraved measuring spoons or cups. For great monogrammed gifts such as steak brands, spatulas, aprons, etc... www.williams-sonoma.com

• If you are having Mexican food for dinner, come home with chips, salsa, fresh limes, and Margarita mix to augment dinner, and consider bringing home a Mariachi Band CD or a potted cactus to offer as appreciation for your partner's effort or as a more lasting reminder of a great evening. If Italian is on the menu, bring home an Italian bottle of wine or pick up an Italian- themed CD to play. Order a real Italian dessert from your local Italian restaurant on your way home to enhance the meal. If you are cooking dinner together, don't forget to spoon feed your significant other tastes of the spaghetti sauce as you fine-tune the spices.

• Go the extra mile ordering dessert at your favorite restaurant, call ahead and ask the chef to personalize your dessert by writing a special message on it for your sweetheart. (There is often no extra charge for this lovely service.)

Know your Wines:

There are tons of wonderful books and Websites that offer tips and facts about wine and wine pairing with food. Whether you are extremely interested in the subject or just looking for minimal advice, this Website offers fantastic free tips on pairing wine with food. Simply select an entrée or sauce and the Website gives you a suggested wine to best complement your meal. They even have a section on the site that pairs wines with frozen dinners, burgers, and popular snacks. www.wineanswers.com

Tips on Selecting Wines:

There are general guidelines that can help even the most unfamiliar wine drinker pair wines successfully with food. I certainly hope that these guidelines will be helpful, however, you should also keep in mind that your taste buds are your own and your food and wine experiences should please them. You should always order and drink what you like.

On the other hand, if you aren't a seasoned wine connoisseur but you are interested in experimenting more in the wine world, try buying or ordering what is suggested. You may be delighted with the discovery!

Although these guidelines are helpful and can be followed on their own, you should never be embarrassed to ask for help when making a wine selection at a store or at a restaurant. Many stores and restaurants have staff members who specialize in wine knowledge and would be delighted to share it with you. At L'Etoile, we educate our wait staff about the wines on our list, and we encourage our servers to try them before recommending them to our guests. Your server may have already tried the wines you are deciding between or have just tasted a dish you are ordering with a particular wine and therefore be in a great position to offer you assistance. After you order wine, your server or the sommelier will bring the bottle (to the person who ordered it), show you the label to confirm that it is the bottle you ordered, uncork it at your table, and pour a sample in your glass. You should swirl the wine around in the glass to expose it to some air, smell the aroma released through swirling, and then taste the wine; if you are pleased with the wine, tell your waiter or simply nod and he/she will pour for your guests and then for you.

In the wine world, it is common to encounter bottles of wine that have spoiled. There are many steps from harvesting the grapes through processing and storage that could lead to a spoiled bottle, long before it arrives at your table. If the wine you are being served tastes off or resembles vinegar, then it may be a spoiled bottle. You should feel free to ask your server about it, if it is in fact spoiled, he/she will bring you another bottle.

Here are some general pairing suggestions that can be used as a starting point. Typically full bodied red wines, such as Cabernet Sauvignon, Pinot Noir, and Merlot, are paired with red meat dishes and most dishes that feature tomato based sauces. Zinfandel, Grenache, and Syrah tend to be bolder with peppery, sometimes spicy flavors; these wines are very versatile and can be used to bring out more flavor in already spicy dishes or to add interest to otherwise simple meals.

In most cases, white wines such as Chardonnay, Sauvignon Blanc, and Viognier, harmonize nicely with chicken, fish, and cream based sauces.

When selecting these wines, you have the option of crisp, dry wines that cleanse the palate and wines that tend to have more oak and butter flavors that enhance the richness of the dish you are serving. Reisling, Muscat, and Gewurtzraminer, are all white wines that range from slightly to very sweet; these wines pair very well with cheese, many salads, and desserts.

Champagne is another wine that is very flexible with food. Naturally people think of champagne when planning romantic evenings, celebrations, and special events. It is great to know that the unique flavor in champagne brings out many subtle flavors in all food; so feel free to pair champagne with any meal you want to serve your sweetheart!

Wine Tasting Guidelines:

The basic characteristics of a wine are appearance, aroma, and taste. When you first pick up a glass of wine, you look to judge its appearance. Is the wine clarity brilliant or a bit hazy? Is there sediment in the wine bottle? The color of the wine, its depth and hue, also play a part in evaluating the wine.

After you look at the wine, you want to swirl it in your glass to release its aroma. Aromas are judged on purity, intensity, and, of course, the individual scents that comprise it. There is a wide range of scents that can be found in wine, floral, fruity, spicy, nutty, woody, earthy, pungent, and chemical scents are all general categories that begin to describe the aroma of wine. When you smell your wine, begin by describing a more general scent and see if you can be more specific as the aroma lingers.

Finally, you taste your wine. In tasting wine there are several aspects of the wine that will likely make an impression. The first is usually the way the wine feels in your mouth - is it rich and full-bodied or more delicate and light-bodied? The flavors of the wine are created by the interaction of several components, first the fruit used in the wine and the area where that fruit was grown, then the fermentation process that made the wine, and finally the age of the wine. As you taste the wine, you will also notice the acidity of the wine; high acid wines tend to taste crisp, sharp, and somewhat sour where low acid wines taste soft and creamy. Once you have tasted the wine, you will also note the complexity of the finish, whether the wine is simple and easy or multi-dimensional and lingering on the palate.

Aphrodisiacs:

Edible aphrodisiacs are foods and beverages that are believed to increase or arouse sexual desire. They were named for Aphrodite, the Greek goddess of love. Aphrodisiacs have been highly valued for centuries around the world. For many civilizations, procreation was of great importance and there were many reasons, like undernourishment, anxiety, and fatigue, that people experienced a loss of libido, so aphrodisiacs were found to encourage sexual desire and promote fertility. There are lots of edible aphrodisiac lists available; some of the most commonly known edible aphrodisiacs are oysters, frog legs, caviar, and truffles. These foods, however, are generally more expensive or more difficult to prepare at home, so it might interest you to know that there are lots of others out there.

Many foods are labeled as aphrodisiacs thanks to their physical resemblance to various body parts; however, there are several reasons beyond visual stimulation that make some foods able to stimulate desire. For example, eating meat fills your blood stream with an amino acid called tyrosine, which helps mental alertness and concentration. Natural sugars found in fresh fruits and juice are metabolized quickly and give you a boost of energy. If your levels of serotonin (a brain chemical that affects your mood) are too low, your libido may suffer, which can be remedied by increasing your intake of carbohydrates. Spices are used to awaken the taste buds, and when served well and with love, they awaken other desires too. If you are really sleepy, eating or drinking something with a little caffeine might get you going or if you are too stressed and preoccupied to enjoy a night with your loved one, having a moderate amount of alcohol might help ... not too much though or you might fall asleep. Some research shows that zinc is linked to fertility and sexual desire and that men who have low levels of zinc in their blood stream may also have a low sperm count ... so gentlemen, find yourselves some seafood, lean meat, beans or just a bowl of cereal! Some foods are labeled as aphrodisiacs because of their cultural heritage and what they symbolize for people around the world. Although this list is not all-inclusive, it does offer you many of the foods that are still used today as aphrodisiacs.

• apricots • artichokes • asparagus • almonds • arugula • avocado • bananas • sweet basil • carrots • celery • chocolate • cilantro • cloves • coffee • cucumber • dates • eggs • fennel • figs • fish • garlic • ginger • grapes • honey • ice cream • lamb • licorice • lobster • mango • mustard • nutmeg • nuts • onions • peaches • pepper • pine nuts • pineapple • pomegranate • quince • raspberries • rice • saffron • strawberries • tequila • tomatoes • unagi • vanilla • wine • zucchini •

Now that you have some basic food and wine knowledge, I hope you will look through these recipes and choose a few to prepare for your loved one. Once you know what you would like to prepare, invite your partner to join you. For example:

Please be my date for a delicious dinner for two.
We have exclusive reservations at 7:00 in a
private dining room,

"Chez Nous" (at our house)!

"Oeufs Cocotte"
Baked Eggs with Toast Points

1. In French cooking this is a classic egg preparation. When I prepare a breakfast in bed, I try to think about how easy the dish is to make and how easy it is to eat ... you don't want it to be messy! To bake Oeufs Cocotte, you will need to have small, oven-safe ramekins; ramekins vary in size although they are generally small, ceramic dishes. This dish can be set up the night before and placed in the hot water bath and baked in the morning.

2. The toast points are a delicious accompaniment and are meant to be dipped into the egg. (I also love to dip sliced, crispy bacon into these eggs!)

Ingredients:

2 eggs

2 buttered ramekins

2 oz of heavy cream

2 pieces of white bread
(with the crusts removed)

1 teaspoon of chives

1 Tablespoon of butter

Method:

Pre-heat your oven to 325°.

Bring the cream to a boil and reduce by half; it will thicken in the process. Remove from the heat and cool the cream for a few minutes. Crack an egg into each buttered ramekin. Sprinkle the egg with a pinch of salt and pepper and pour the cream over the egg. (At this point the ramekins can be covered and refrigerated until you are ready to bake them in the morning, they can be made up to a day ahead.)

Place the ramekins into a casserole dish and fill the casserole dish halfway with hot water. Place in the pre-heated oven and bake for about 15 minutes or until the whites are just set. Remove from the oven, top each egg with chives and serve with the toast points.

For the toast points, cut bread slices into 4 triangles. Heat a frying pan on low. Add the butter and when it is all melted and bubbly, add the triangles. Brown them slowly on both sides, serve immediately.

Baked French Toast with Rum Caramel and Bananas

This is another recipe that can be prepared the night before you want to serve it. You can assemble the French toast in ramekins; ramekins vary in size although they are generally small, ceramic dishes. Bake them in the same water bath as the "Oeufs Cocotte," though the French toast will take longer, so you will want to start those ramekins first and halfway through baking the French toast add the egg dishes. Any kind of bread works well for this recipe, although brioche is ideal. If you or your partner have a favorite bread, that will work just fine.

For the French Toast

Ingredients:

2 thick slices of bread (approx. 1 inch)

1 egg

½ cup of milk

1 teaspoon of vanilla

1 pinch of cinnamon

1 pinch of nutmeg

1 pinch of allspice

1 Tablespoon of brown sugar

Method:

Use the ramekin as a "cutter" and cut out a circle in the center of each of the slices of bread. Whisk all of the ingredients together in a bowl and dip each circle of bread into the bowl, make sure you allow the bread to soak up some of the liquid. Cook the bread circles in a frying pan with a little oil until they brown on both sides. Butter two ramekins and place a circle of French toast in the bottom of each.

For the Bananas

Ingredients:

1 Tablespoon of butter

2 Tablespoons of brown sugar

1 banana

1 or 2 oz of rum or brandy

1 pinch of cinnamon

fresh berries (sliced strawberries, raspberries, blueberries, etc.)

maple syrup

Method:

In a frying pan, heat the butter and the brown sugar and stir to combine them. When the mixture is caramel colored and bubbly, remove it from the heat and add the rum. Bring the mixture back to a boil; then add the cinnamon and slices of the banana. Toss the bananas through the caramel and place them on top of the toast in the ramekins. At this point, the ramekins can be covered and refrigerated over night and then baked in the morning.

Pre-heat your oven to 325°.

Place your ramekins in a casserole dish and fill the dish halfway with hot water. Cover the casserole dish with aluminum foil and bake for 20 minutes or until it is warmed through. Top each ramekin with your choice of fresh berries and a drizzle of maple syrup.

Blueberry Scones

Warm scones, fresh from the oven, served with butter and coffee or juice make a great breakfast in bed. This recipe is so easy that you can enjoy these scones any time. Have fun with the flavors too. Blueberries are my favorite, but these would be great with raspberries, blackberries, chocolate chips, or chopped nuts. Simply substitute the one cup of fresh blueberries for one cup of the ingredient of your choice.

Ingredients:

(Makes 8 scones)

2 cups of all-purpose flour

3 teaspoons baking powder

1/4 cup of sugar

1/3 cup unsalted butter

3/4 cup of half and half

1 egg yolk

1 cup of fresh blueberries

Method:

Pre-heat your oven to 425°. Sift the flour, baking powder, and sugar into a bowl.

Cut the butter into small cubes and place them into the freezer for 10 minutes. Add the butter to the flour mixture and use a pastry cutter or your fingers to quickly work the butter into the flour until the mixture resembles fine crumbs.

Beat the egg and the half and half together, then add the mixture to the dry ingredients. Mix the wet and dry ingredients together until the whole mixture is just moistened. Gently fold in the blueberries.

Turn the dough out onto a floured surface and knead gently to form a ball. Press the dough into a circle about 3/4 of an inch thick, then place it on a greased baking sheet. Using a knife, score the dough into 8 wedges. Do not cut all the way through. Sprinkle with sugar and bake for about 20 minutes or until brown. Break the circle into wedges, dust the pieces with powdered sugar, and serve warm (preferably with butter!).

Crisp Vegetable Salad with Sesame-Soy Vinaigrette

I love this salad; it is simple, colorful, crunchy, and delicious. The vinaigrette can be made well in advance and stored in the refrigerator until you are ready to serve.

For the Salad

Ingredients:

1 red bell pepper

1 yellow bell pepper

1 orange bell pepper

1 small jicama

1 small daikon radish

1 carrot

1 English cucumber

1 handful of enoki mushrooms (optional)

1 bunch of cilantro (stems removed and leaves reserved)

salt and pepper

Method:

To prepare the vegetables, I make a cut called a Julienne. This is done by cutting the vegetable into a square and then into thin slices and finally into "match stick" size strips. For this salad, the key is to cut the vegetables into small, easy to eat pieces. Place all of your cut vegetables into a large mixing bowl and toss them with the cilantro leaves. Sprinkle with a pinch of salt and pepper. Dress the vegetables with the vinaigrette, remembering to mix well.

For the Vinaigrette

Ingredients:

2 Tablespoons rice wine vinegar

1 Tablespoon soy sauce

1 Tablespoon honey

1 teaspoon toasted seasame oil

1 Tablespoon fresh ginger (chopped fine)

1 Tablespoon fresh shallot (chopped fine)

pinch of crushed red pepper flakes

3/4 cup of grape seed oil

Method:

Whisk all of the ingredients in a bowl and reserve.

Plating the Salad

As you can see in the picture, I like to present this salad in the center of a circle of thinly sliced cucumbers. First place the cucumber slices around the edge of the plate, then place the dressed salad in the center of the circle. Garnish the salad with some toasted sesame seeds or a few fresh cilantro leaves. Then you are ready to serve.

Spicy Shrimp Bisque

This soup is silky, creamy, and rich. The tomatoes and wine add a great balance and depth to the flavor. This soup is at its best when it is made with fresh heirloom tomato varieties; Brandy wines, Amish Paste, and Black Krim are my favorite varieties for this soup. If these are unavailable you can substitute canned tomatoes.

Ingredients:

1 pound of shrimp (peeled and veined)

1 small onion

2 stalks of celery

1 carrot

2 cloves of garlic

1 fennel bulb

2 Tablespoons of olive oil

2 cups of tomatoes

1 cup of sauvignon blanc

pinch of red pepper flakes

pinch of cayenne

salt and pepper

2 bay leaves

1 cup of heavy cream

4 cups of fish broth (substitute chicken or vegetable broth)

1 Tablespoon of chopped parsley

Method:

Begin by chopping your onion, celery, carrot, garlic, and fennel. You do not need to worry about being fancy when you chop these, since the soup will be puréed.

Heat a heavy bottomed stock pot on medium. Add the olive oil and all of the vegetables except for the tomatoes. Season the vegetables with salt and pepper and sweat them for about 3 minutes. Add the tomatoes and cayenne and chili flakes. Add the wine and the bay leaves and simmer for about 5 minutes. Add the stock and cook for about 20-30 minutes. Add the cream and simmer for 5 minutes. Add the shrimp and simmer for 2 minutes. Remove 4-6 shrimp from the soup and slice them in half. Save these shrimp pieces for garnish. Place the soup in a blender and purée until smooth.

To Serve:

Ladle the soup into a bowl. Place the reserved shrimp in the middle of the bowl and top with chopped parsley and drizzle with a little olive oil.

Sweet Corn Chowder with Crab

This is one of my favorite soups in the summer. You should make the corn stock; it is well worth the extra effort! You can freeze what you don't use, or use it in the halibut dish.

For the Soup Base

Ingredients:

4 cloves of garlic

2 small onions

3 Yukon gold potatoes

4 cups corn stock

1 cup heavy cream

1 dozen ears of corn
(corn removed and cobs reserved)

4 oz butter

Method:

Sweat garlic and onions in the butter for about 3 minutes. Add the corn stock and potatoes. Bring to a boil, then add the cream and the corn, reserving one cup for garnish. Simmer for about 15 minutes. Purée and set aside.

For the Corn Stock

Ingredients:

1 dozen corn cobs

3 onions

3 stalks celery

1 head garlic

1 bunch fresh thyme

1 Tablespoon whole black peppercorns

2 bay leaves

8 cups water

Method:

Add all ingredients to a large stock pot and bring to a boil. Reduce heat and simmer for about 1½ hours. Strain and reserve.

For the Garnish

Ingredients:

8 oz. crab meat

1 cup corn

3 oz. bacon (optional)

1 Tablespoon butter

Method:

Render the bacon until brown and crisp. Add the butter and corn and sauté for about 2 minutes. Add the crab and toss through until warm.

To Serve:

Place a small amount of garnish in the center of a bowl and slowly add the soup so the garnish stays in place. Top with a few leaves of cilantro or parsley.

Lamb Chops with Chèvre and Beet Risotto

The beets are the important part of the risotto, adding the pink color to the rice. Roasting beets enhances the sweetness while reducing the "earthy" qualities some beets may have. I love to add to the presentation of this dish by taking a heart shaped cookie cutter, filling it with the risotto and using a spoon to fill in the shape as illustrated below.

For the Lamb Chops

Ingredients:

2-4 lamb chops

salt and pepper

2 sprigs of rosemary

1 clove of garlic

olive oil for searing

Method:

Pre-heat your oven to 400°. Season each chop on both sides with salt and pepper. Heat an oven-safe skillet or frying pan on high. Add about 2 Tablespoons of olive oil and lower the heat to medium-high. Place the chops in the pan and brown them on both sides, for approximately 2-3 minutes on each side. Add the garlic and rosemary and place the skillet in the oven and roast for about 12 minutes. Remove the lamb chops from the pan and rest them on a plate for 5 minutes before serving.

Roasted Beets

Ingredients:

2-3 red beets

water

salt and pepper

2 Tablespoons of vegetable oil or olive oil

Method:

Pre-heat your oven to 325°. Wash the beets and place them in a casserole or metal baking dish. Add water just to cover the bottom of the dish. Add the oil and sprinkle with salt and pepper. Cover the dish with aluminum foil and roast for about 45 minutes or until tender.

For the Risotto

Ingredients:

2 Tablespoons olive oil

½ of an onion (minced)

1 clove of garlic (minced)

1 cup of Arborio rice

4-5 cups chicken or vegetable stock

1 cup of white wine

1 cup of roasted beets

4 Tablespoons fresh chèvre

Truffle oil (optional)

1 Tablespoon butter

Method:

Bring the stock to a boil; then turn down the heat but keep the stock simmering. In a separate heavy bottomed sauce pot, heat the olive oil on medium. Add the onion and garlic and simmer for about 3 minutes. Add the wine and simmer until almost all of the wine has evaporated. Add the rice and stir. Add 1 cup of the simmering broth and stir until the rice has absorbed the liquid. Repeat until the rice is tender. Add the beets and stir through. Add the chèvre and butter and stir until they are melted and creamy. Drizzle with the truffle oil and serve.

Serving this Dish:

When plating your food, place the risotto in the center of the plate and put one or two lamb chops around it and leaning onto the pile of risotto. Place a sprig of rosemary or parsley in the top of the risotto. Adding a drizzle of olive oil to the plate is an elegant touch and adds a bit of flair.

Seared Tuna with Olive Oil, Crushed Potatoes, Asparagus and Whole Grain Mustard Vinaigrette

After a long winter, the asparagus is finally in season around the end of April. This dish is great, light, and delicious. The tuna and asparagus can be grilled if you have one, but are also great done this way. The combination of the olive oil, slow cooked onions, asparagus, and mustard take this very simple dish to a much higher level.

Ingredients:

2 tuna steaks

1 bunch of asparagus

2-3 Yukon gold potatoes

1 onion

1 cup of olive oil

salt and pepper

For the Vinaigrette

Ingredients:

1 egg yolk

1 Tablespoon whole grain mustard

2 Tablespoons of white wine vinegar

2 Tablespoons water

1 shallot (minced)

½ cup of vegetable oil

½ cup of olive oil

salt and pepper

1 Tablespoon of chopped parsley

Method:

In a bowl, whisk the egg yolk, vinegar, water, mustard, and shallot. When foamy, slowly drizzle in the oils. Season and finish with parsley.

For the Potatoes

Method:

In a small sauce pan place the thinly sliced onion and olive oil and season with salt and pepper. Heat on low, cook for about an hour or until the onions are completely translucent and soft. Remove from the heat and set aside.

Cut the potatoes into fairly evenly sized pieces. Put in a pot and cover with water, then season liberally with salt. Bring just to a boil and turn the heat down. Cook for about a ½ hour or until they are fork tender. Drain and place in a large bowl. Add the onion and olive oil mixture and smash them together. Season with salt and pepper.

For the Asparagus

Method:

Bring a pot of water, big enough to hold all of your asparagus, to a boil with enough salt in it to make it taste like ocean water. While the water is coming to a boil wash and snap your asparagus. (Asparagus naturally is woody and tough at its base; to remove that part of the stem, hold the asparagus with one end in each hand and slowly apply pressure to bend the asparagus, like you were folding it in half. The asparagus stem will snap off where the woody part ends and the part remaining with the tip will be tender.) Fill a large bowl with ice water and have it standing by. Blanch and shock the asparagus by placing it in the boiling water and boiling until the asparagus is bright green, about 1 minute. Remove from the boiling water and place the asparagus directly into the ice water.

For the Tuna

Method:

In the restaurant we use an iron skillet to sear the tuna, if you don't have one you can use a frying pan.

Season the fish on all sides with salt and pepper. On one side, touch a knife to the fish so that it makes a slight cut, but do not slice, just gently score the fish. (This will make it easier to slice after it is seared.) If you are using a frying pan add a few tablespoons of oil, when your pan is hot place the fish in, scored side down. Sear quickly on both sides, remove and slice.

Serve with a dollop of the crushed potatoes, heat the asparagus with a little boiling water and put on the plate. Place the sliced tuna right on top. Have fun with the vinegar. Put it in a squeeze bottle and make a design or just drizzle over the fish.

Fried Eggplant Napoleon served with Fresh Mozzarella, Ratatouille and Balsamic Reduction

This colorful, simple dish is one of my favorites because it is so versatile. It works wonderfully as a delicious vegetarian entree, but it is also fantastic with fresh fish, like snapper, as well as with a grilled steak or chicken breast.

For the Eggplant

Ingredients:

1 eggplant

1 ball of fresh mozzarella

1 cup of bread crumbs

1/4 cup of parmesan cheese

1 teaspoon of chopped parsley

1 egg and a splash of water

flour for dredging

oil for frying

Method:

Peel and slice the eggplant into 1/4 inch slices. Mix the bread crumbs with the parmesan and parsley. Set up a bowl with flour, a bowl with the egg and water (egg wash), and a bowl with the bread crumb mixture. Place a slice of eggplant into the flour and coat well. Shake off the excess flour and place the eggplant slice into the egg wash. Let the excess egg wash drip off and then place the eggplant slice into the breading mixture and make sure to coat it on all sides. Repeat the breading process until you have coated each slice of eggplant first with flour, then with egg wash and finally with the bread crumb mixture. Store the slices of eggplant, covered, in the refrigerator.

Cut the mozzarella into 1/8 inch slices. When you are ready to serve, heat about an 1/8 of an inch of vegetable oil in a frying pan. Dip a slice of the eggplant in, if it sizzles the oil is ready and you can begin frying. If it doesn't, wait a few minutes and try again. You only want to turn the eggplant once in the pan, so wait until you see some browning on the edges of each piece, then flip the slice and continue cooking until the slice is golden brown. Remove the eggplant from the oil, season it with salt and pepper, and top each slice with a slice of the fresh mozzarella. The idea is to have a small stack of eggplant, cheese, eggplant, cheese and finally eggplant for each plate.

For the Ratatouille

Ingredients:

1 zucchini squash (green)

1 yellow squash

1 red onion

1 red bell pepper

1 teaspoon herbs de provence

1/4 cup of olive oil

2 cloves of garlic

1 cup of balsamic vinegar

1 teaspoon red wine vinegar

salt and pepper

Method:

Dice the squash, zucchini, bell pepper, and red onion. Chop the garlic. Heat the olive oil on medium-high. Add the vegetables and quickly sauté. Lower the heat and season the vegetables with the herbs de provence, salt and pepper. Add the red wine vinegar and cook until the vegetables are al dente.

Bring the one cup of balsamic vinegar to a simmer and reduce until it is about 1/4 of a cup. Cool and drizzle it around the plate with a little of the olive oil that you cooked the ratatouille in.

Amazing additions to this dish would be olive tapenade and tomato fondue. If you are feeling ambitious, I would encourage you to give these recipes a try.

For the Tomato Fondue

Ingredients:

4 roma tomatoes

1 clove of garlic

1 shallot minced

1 sprig of fresh thyme

1/4 cup of olive oil

Method:

Bring a pot of water to a boil. Remove the core from the tomatoes and make a small x in the opposite end. Place the tomatoes into the boiling water for about 10 seconds. Remove from the boiling water and run under cold water to remove the skin. Cut the tomatoes in half and remove the seeds. Then roughly chop the tomatoes and place them into a pot with the olive oil, garlic, shallot, and thyme. Bring to a simmer on low, low heat. Cook for about an hour, stirring occasionally, until all of the tomatoes have "melted" and most of the liquid has cooked out.

For the Olive Tapenade

Ingredients:

1 cup of nicoise olives (pits removed)

1 Tablespoon of capers

1 clove of garlic

2 Tablespoons of olive oil

1 Tablespoon of chopped parsley

Method:

If you have a food processor, place all of the ingredients in and pulse. If you don't, chop all the ingredients and mix them with the olive oil in a bowl.

Place a spoonful of the tomato fondue and the olive tapenade either directly on top of the eggplant napoleon or just set a spoonful of each on the plate.

Cornmeal Crusted Halibut served with Sweet Corn and Chanterelle Mushrooms in a White Wine Cream Sauce

I love this combination of sweet corn and chanterelles. The cornmeal crust helps keep the halibut from breaking apart while cooking. The overall dish is easy and delicious for the summer. I like to serve it with simple mashed potatoes.

Sweet Corn and Chanterelle Mushroom Sauce

Ingredients:

3 cups of white wine (sauvignon blanc)

2 shallots (minced)

4 cloves of garlic (minced)

2 cups of corn stock
(*see corn chowder recipe)

½ cup cream

2 oz. butter

1 cup corn

5 oz. chanterelle mushrooms

1 Tablespoon chopped chive and parsley

Method:

Place wine, shallots, and garlic in a pot. Bring to a boil and reduce until almost all of the liquid is gone. Add corn stock, bring to a boil, and reduce by half. Add cream and corn, and then simmer for about 5 minutes. Sweat mushrooms in the butter until soft and add to the sauce. (Sweating is a technique often used with vegetables, where they are placed in a small amount of fat, covered and cooked over low heat, softening the vegetables and cooking them in their own juices without browning them.)

For the Cornmeal Savory Crust Halibut

Ingredients:

2 halibut steaks

1 cup corn meal

1 cup bread crumbs

2 Tablespoons chopped summer savory (optional)

1 egg

salt and pepper

about 2 Tablespoons of vegetable oil

Method:

Pre-heat your oven to 400°. Whip the egg in one bowl. In another bowl, combine the cornmeal, bread crumbs and savory if you are using it. Dip the halibut steaks on one side in the egg and then into the dry ingredients. Season the fish with salt and pepper. Heat an oven safe frying pan on medium heat. Add the vegetable oil to coat the pan and place the fish in the pan with the crusted side down. When the fish is "sizzling" put the whole pan into the oven for about 8-12 minutes. Do not flip the fish until you are ready to serve. When ready serve the fish on top of the mushroom and corn sauce.

Dark Chocolate Cake with Warm Chocolate Sauce

This chocolate cake with warm chocolate sauce is sexy on so many levels. The cake is always moist and the addition of the sauce puts the dessert over the top! It goes best with a scoop of you and your partner's favorite ice cream. If you have fresh berries, they are a perfect garnish for this dessert. Although this dessert is simple, it is decadent and delicious. Serve a big piece of the cake in the center of the plate and pour the sauce on top of it just before serving.

For the Cake

Ingredients:

1¾ cups all-purpose flour

¾ cup cocoa powder

2 cups granulated sugar

1½ teaspoons baking soda

1½ teaspoons baking powder

1 teaspoon salt

2 eggs

1 cup milk

½ cup oil

2 teaspoons vanilla

1 cup boiling water

Method:

Sift the flour and cocoa together; then combine all the dry ingredients together.

Add the eggs, milk, oil, and vanilla to the dry ingredients and beat for 2 minutes.

Stir in the boiling water; then pour the batter into two greased and lined 9 inch pans.

Bake the cake at 350° for 30-35 minutes.

Do not over bake; the cake is done when it pulls away from the sides of the pan. A tester inserted in the center of the cake will have moist crumbs attached to it when removed.

Let the cake cool in the pan for 10 minutes. Remove from the pan and let the cake finish cooling on a wire rack. Note: This is a sticky, moist cake. It is best to rest it in the fridge for a few hours before cutting.

For the Chocolate Sauce

Ingredients:

8 oz. bittersweet chocolate chips

½ cup light corn syrup

approx. 1 to 2 cups of milk

Method:

Heat the chocolate chips and corn syrup in a double boiler until the chocolate is melted and smooth. Remove from the heat and whisk in milk until you reach the desired consistency. It should fall in a steady stream when poured from a spoon over the cake.

Blueberry Crisp

Blueberries may be my favorite thing about the summer and this crisp is a perfect way to show off delicious in-season blueberries! This crisp is great when served warm with a scoop of vanilla ice cream or a dollop of sweet whipped cream or crème fraîche. The crisp topping is very versatile and can be used to top any variety or combination of fruit in the filling, like apple, rhubarb, strawberry, etc. It is also delicious on its own!

For the Blueberry Filling

Ingredients:

1 pint blueberries

½ cup sugar

juice from ½ a lemon

1 Tablespoon corn starch

Method:

Mix all the ingredients and set aside.

For the Crisp Streusel Topping

Ingredients:

1 stick unsalted butter

1/3 cup brown sugar

½ cup oats

2/3 cup all purpose flour

¼ Tablespoon baking powder

¼ teaspoon salt

Method:

Cream the butter and sugar. Add the baking powder and salt and beat until combined. Stir in the oats and flour. Spread this mixture in a cookie sheet and bake at 400° for 10 minutes. Stir the mixture, spread it out again and then bake for 5 more minutes. When done the mixture should be light brown and a little crisp. Allow the topping to cool.

For Assembly:

Place the blueberry mixture into a baking dish, if you have individual ramekins or baking dishes they are great for bringing the dish right from the oven to the table. Crumble the topping over the blueberry mixture and bake at 400° for about 10 minutes. Garnish with ice cream, powdered sugar, and a sprig of fresh mint.

Espresso Chocolate Mousse

Chocolate mousse is easy, yet decadent. You can use dark, milk, or white chocolate to make this mousse, although my personal favorite is dark chocolate. This mousse serves beautifully in wine glasses, especially if you layer whipped cream between the layers of mousse. A light dusting of cocoa is always a nice finishing touch; additionally, raspberries make a delicious and beautiful garnish for this dessert. This is a great dessert to make in advance; they will keep well in the refrigerator for 2-3 days before serving.

Ingredients:

4 ½ oz. dark chocolate

2 Tablespoons butter

2 Tablespoons Tia Maria (or coffee liquor)

1 cup whipping cream

3 eggs (separated)

1 Tablespoon sugar

1 Tablespoon powdered sugar

Method:

In a double boiler, slowly melt the chocolate with the butter and Tia Maria. Whisk until smooth and remove from heat.

Whip the cream with the powdered sugar until stiff peaks form. (You know you have made stiff peaks, when you remove the whisk and turn it upside down and the cream makes a little "peak" without falling over.)

Whip the whites to soft peak with the sugar.

The chocolate is ready to use when it has cooled to just above body temperature. (Test this by placing a small amount on a spoon and touching it to your lower lip, if it feels warm that's good, if it feels hot stir for a minute and try again.)

Whisk the egg yolks over a double boiler until they are light and frothy. Once frothy, cool the egg yolks to the touch, but do not let them get cold. Then fold the yolks into the chocolate.

Fold in the beaten egg whites and then the whipped cream.

Place in serving bowls and chill for about 8 hours.

For those who lack the time, energy, or inclination to prepare elaborate meals from scratch, a way to cheat just a touch is to visit Web sites such as www.alazing.com or www.impromptugourmet.com.

The frozen meals require normal preparation, but are scrumptious and simple. It can be your little secret!

Sgt. Traci's
Arsenal of Romantic Ideas

“Fairy tales are filled with characters who dream of loving the way we do.”

–Sgt. Traci

These romantic gifts and ideas are meant to pique your imagination and inspire you to try something different in your relationship that will ultimately enhance other areas in your life. "Time-outs" from the rest of the world that are spent re-connecting with your partner are an integral key to maintaining and sustaining a long-lasting, loving relationship.

Many of these ideas are my own that I have done, had done for me, or will eventually do for someone. Others, I heard, saw, or read about and liked enough to share. Some of these ideas may seem off the wall, out of reach, expensive, surreal, unrealistic, or just plain dumb to you. And that's okay, but I hope you will try some of them anyway. The sobering reality is that everything will eventually die without nourishment, including relationships. If you currently feel like you have a mediocre relationship or love life, it may be that you aren't providing enough of the proper "nourishment" that your relationship needs to survive. Before your relationship fades into the mundane or worse, remember that everything begins and ends with you and you can take control back. The old saying definitely applies, "you can't continue to do what you've been doing and expect to get different results." So if you are looking for different results for your love life, try some of these different ideas and watch what happens!

Table of Contents

Novelty Ideas

1. Through the years. Have an "age enhanced" picture or painting made from a photo of the two of you. The picture should depict a sense of a long, happy, and fulfilled life together. "Together until the end." There you are, sitting side by side in your rocking chairs, reminiscing through an old photo album of days gone by.

2. Are they entitled? Buy a novelty Title of sentiment from Britain for your loved one. Choose from the following: Lord, Lady, Laird, Baron, Baroness, Earl, Count, Countess, Viscount, Marquis, Marchioness, Duke, Duchess, Sir, Madame, and others. This novel gift idea is authentic looking. It is perfect for the person who has everything, including a big head!
www.elitetitles.co.uk

3. Up in Arms. Another neat gift idea is to have a family "Coat of Arms" framed or embossed on something. There are many different options and ornamentations from which to choose.
www.surnamehistories.com

4. Pretty crafty. Handcraft something for your partner. One idea would be to make a milestone scrapbook or photo album that captures the jubilant moments of your partner's life or of your relationship together.

5. Emeril live. Take cooking lessons and prepare and serve your honey a really special meal. I recently saw an interview where Shaquille O'Neal rented an entire restaurant and hired the chef to teach him how to prepare his wife's favorite meal. Shaq, in romantic fashion, served his wife in chef's attire and personally waited on her every desire.

6. Pretty crafty. Join him in his craft, skill, or trade and create something together. I had taken a two part woodworking lesson so that I could make an inscribed Koa wooden clock for my (former) fiancé giving him the gift of "time." I had the instructor take photos during each step of the process of my "labor of love" all the way through to the final stages of staining. I made a little booklet using the photos of my blood, sweat, and tears during the making of the clock, and I recorded a collage of my thoughts during the course and woodworking process.

I wrapped the booklet as a gift itself and presented it with the inscribed "forever in time... with you" clock.

7. Color her world. Another time, I hired an artist friend to help me duplicate a life-like version of my favorite painting by Jim Warren, replacing the face from the artist's original, with that of my best friend. I added many personalized touches depicting the earrings in her ears and necklace around her neck as jewelry I had given to her throughout our twenty years of friendship. In between the countless hours of the artist's lessons, teachings, and assistance, he snapped photographs of me each time that I braved small painting additions to help personalize the re-created masterpiece. I mailed the beautifully framed gift to her to arrive just in time for Thanksgiving, a small token of my appreciation to commemorate the beautiful gift of the best friendship that I have ever had.

8. Gold medal. My friend's husband did his fair share of "screwing up" throughout the years of their marriage, and being "romantic" was the last of his character traits. One day when they were horseback riding on their farmland, he surprised her with a cheese and cracker and bottle of wine style picnic in the middle of their open field among the wildflowers. He presented her with a gold medal that he had engraved at a trophy shop. One side of the metal awarded his wife "first place" for tolerating all the years of his mischief and on the other side was his briefly inscribed commitment for a new beginning. This simple and inexpensive gesture, meant more to her than all the gifts combined throughout their 20 years of marriage.

9. It's in his kiss (or hers). Pull the sheets down each night and lay a chocolate mint or kiss on the pillow.

10. Something seems fishy. This idea is from the youthful days of my first big crush. Buy a small glass fish bowl and two fish. Name the fish after you and your crush. Then cut out a heart and write out names on it. Tape it on the back of the glass. Mine read "Traci & Kie, together forever."

11. Bottled emotions. Tear bottles have spanned the ages as a tender tradition of shared emotions and transformed relationships. A

treasured gift for three millennia, some tear bottles have held real tears of joy, sorrow, or forgiveness; others have symbolized those feelings. When you give this special gift to honor and cherish another person, it conveys your shared grief or celebrated joy or requests essential forgiveness or expresses unconditional love. Shedding tears for someone you love is an incredibly intimate expression of affection. Washington Irving may have said it best when he said, "There is sacredness in tears. They are not the mark of weakness but of power. They speak more eloquently than ten thousand tongues. They are the messengers of overwhelming grief, of deep contrition, and of unspeakable love." www.timelesstraditionsgifts.com (Mention coupon code R0206 and receive a 10% discount.)

12. Forever on my heart. Have a palm sized portrait or profile of your partner tattooed near your heart. While I am not personally a fan of body art, you may be. I have a friend who surprised his wife in this fashion and I must admit that it is surprisingly beautiful. Another friend is not allowed to wear a wedding ring at his job for safety reasons, so to honor his wife and commitment to her, he had a classy life-like gold diamond studded wedding ring tattooed in its place. Now, if that isn't romantic, I don't know what is! The wedding band gesture was nothing short of impressive and looks remarkably real!

13. Blanketed in love. Have a quilt made for your partner so he can wrap himself in the warmth of your memories together. On each square, list a single favorite memory. Add a periodic photo print using your favorite photographs throughout the quilt. Example: One square would read: Alaska, another would read: 30th birthday, road trip, camping, country bicycle ride, comedy club, Hawaii, dinner at Spinners, and then there would be a photo of your wedding day...

14. Love on the move. Have your license plates personalized with your partner's name, his/ her "pet" name, or each of your initials.

15. I just called to say I Love You. Set "your song" on your cell phone as the ring tone each time your sweetheart calls.

16. Bottled up emotions. Have a commemorating message delivered to your partner. I appreciate the masterful elegance of a timeless message in a bottle and have personal experience with this company. www.timelessmessage.com

17. Unlock the doors. Choose from a truly captivating and extra ordinary collection of Sentimental Messages in a bottle that arrives with a solid, pewter "Key to My Heart." This gift is distinctive, elegant, and will be a sentimental reminder of your time together. The key is actually a copy of a Victorian era gate key which is reminiscent of a simpler, romantic age when these keys opened the gates to beautiful Victorian gardens and homes. The key ring itself can be easily removed for your gift recipient to cherish. They can use it as a key ring or perhaps they may want to keep it with the bottle as a sentimental reminder of your thoughtfulness and love. Choose one of their poems or personalize this special gift by writing your own poem or letter. Each bottle gift is made to order and no two are alike! Offering a one-of-a-kind gift your recipient is sure to treasure for years to come. www.sentimentalmessages.com

18. Key to my heart. Buy one, engrave one, and give one. Through the years, I have collected and tightly clung onto a couple miniature charm-style keys that I have set aside to one day present to the one with whom I will share my heart and my life. First is a sterling silver "key" that will be gifted when the time is right with a card that will read, "He who holds this key can open my heart." Next, reserved especially for my wedding day, is the more elegant 24 kt. gold key. The accompanying card will read "He who holds this key *has* opened my heart." A custom picture frame with an inlaid heart shaped photo of us and an embroidery that reads "...And You Hold the Key." Will be included.

19. Keyed up. Not living together? Are you both ready? Have your house key duplicated or even better, duplicated in sterling silver or gold. Have it engraved with something like "Welcome to our home" or "You have already moved into my heart, please move into our home." Wrap it in a box and present it to him/her (do not use a ring sized box as you may disappoint her if she is hoping for a ring!) After he/she opens it, drop down on your left knee (or both knees, like you really mean it) and ask "Will you move in with me?" This is sweet and romantic and will give you a little practice before doing the real thing. You may have to explain that this is a big step for you. If this goes well, the next step requires just one knee.

20. Label me. A neat romantic gift idea to consider when preparing to ask your partner to move in with you is to wrap up and give him/her return address labels that display both of your names together at the intended new address.

21. Music to her ears. The San Francisco Music Box Company offers a large assortment of masculine, feminine, and themed music and jewelry boxes. SFMBC is working on offering a new service in the near future that will allow you to personalize your music box from a selected list of songs, perhaps "your song" or your partner's favorite song will play each time that he or she opens it. Place a small gift inside for him or her to discover. 1-800-227-2190 – www.sfmusicbox.com

22. Picture this. There is a plethora of photo gift ideas that you can have personalized for your partner. Wal-Mart offers a number of them at reasonable price.

- Calendars
- Mouse pads
- T-shirts
- Sweatshirts
- Playing cards
- Christmas ornaments
- Note cubes
- Ceramic mugs
- Plates
- Puzzles

23. Calendar girl/boy. Have a personalized calendar made with your twelve favorite photos gracing each month. Go the extra mile and write one thing that you love, admire and appreciate about your partner on each square. This way, there will never be a day that your partner doesn't know how you feel about him/her.

24. Familiar faces. Have your favorite photo inlaid on a quilt, blanket, pillow, necktie, purse, or any piece of clothing. There are many other neat gift ideas.
www.personalcreations.com

25. The bark park. There are also unique gift ideas for pets and pet lovers. Impress your partner by bringing his or her beloved pet a small gift or treat or suggest that the two of you take his or her cat or dog on a romantic stroll together. This is a great Web site for ideas.
www.petsnap.com

26. You were framed. Have your favorite love-letter framed or have both of your baby pictures framed side by side with your wedding invitation or wedding vows separating the two of you. Perhaps include your locks of hair or your first baby curls beneath the glass of the frame.

27. Full of hot air. Fill the bathroom with heaps of balloons, writing on each of them with a marker, listing all the reasons your love means so much to you. Add a few redeemable coupons scrolled inside of the balloons or write them directly on the balloon itself with a marker. You could also mail a gift-box with the same intent, this time using helium balloons so they will rise up when he or she opens the package.

28. A SPAtacular day! One of my favorite Birthday gifts was from my best friend Amy who was working as a traveling Physical Therapist in Texas where I was celebrating my birthday. I awoke on the day of my birthday and made my way to the bathroom to find the above listed scenario of a bathroom full of colorful balloons with all kinds of neat messages written on them and on the bathroom mirror of what my day would bring. There was a note telling me to be ready at a certain time in order redeem the rest of my birthday gift. When she arrived back at the apartment to get me, she walked me across the parking lot to the Physical Therapy department where she worked. Because it was a weekend, it was closed for business, and I stepped inside to the sound of my favorite music of the Beatles, the aroma from my favorite scented candles, and the taste of my ready-made favorite beverage. She had set up little "spa" treatment stations, uncovering them as we went along so I couldn't steal a peek of what surprises were yet to come. She treated me with a warm foot bath, followed by a hot paraffin hand wax treatment and then a Paraffin foot wax, a gentle facial-like massage, and the grand finale was one of her famed hour long massages! When she was finished, she ran ahead to the apartment, while I dressed, threw in a pizza, prepared my favorite dessert (apple crisp), and put in my favorite movie. My birthday celebration lasted deep into the night as we talked and laughed for hours in true slumber-party-fashion. It remains one of my most memorable and treasured birthdays ever!

29. A lifetime supply of kisses. Place a single Hershey's kiss wrapped in gold foil in the bottom of a red velvet box (available at most card outlet stores) then add 364 red or silver wrapped Hershey's kisses atop and deliver it to your honey's office. Include a love note stating that this is a lifetime supply of kisses and when they run out, you will replace them for the rest of her life with real ones. Indicate that when he or she reaches the gold foiled kiss it is time to turn it in and redeem it for a fresh supply of kisses for the year. Steal that lone golden-kiss from your sweetie, literally, as a form of redemption for a fresh supply, before refilling the velvet box.

30. Sealed with a kiss. Mail a single Hershey's kiss or hug inside of a tiny box. Enclose a note that says, "Thought you could use one of these," or "I just couldn't wait until you got home." If one kiss isn't enough to satisfy your sweetie, take all the red foiled kisses and make a big shaped heart in the front yard with both your initials inside. I bet this would bring a smile to his/her face when he/she arrives home and sees the special treat awaiting. To avoid ants and the hot sun melting your kisses away, time your placement to coincide in conjunction with your partner's arrival. Also note that if you freeze the foiled kisses, they will take a little longer to melt.

31. My sweet-heart. My brother-in-law is a supervisor at a plastic's company; on one slow night he hand-molded a heart-shaped box for my sister and filled it with Hershey's Kisses, sealed it up nicely, and left it for her to find. When she removed the sealed-wrap and opened the candy box there atop a bed of kisses was a handwritten love-letter. The heart-felt gesture was as beautiful as his words.

32. I want to kiss you all over. Blow 1,000 kisses into a decorative box and wrap it beautifully and deliver with a love-letter. While the box will appear empty to everyone else, the two of you will know what lies within and your partner will think only of you each time that he looks at it.

33. Glass kiss. Give a kiss that will last forever. Glass kisses are the same petite size as a real chocolate candy kiss. Each hand-blown glass kiss is emblazoned with a crimson heart and a personal message tag. What a unique keepsake, tree ornament, or Mother's Day necklace charm. www.timelesstraditionsgifts.com (Mention coupon code R0206 and receive a 10% discount.)

34. Get into their genes. Hire a genealogist to research your partner's heritage and present a framed version of his or her "Family Tree." www.mdarchives.state.md.us/msa/refserv/forms/html/genealogistlist. www.expertgenealogy.com

35. A manicured heart. The next time that you mow the lawn, mow everything around a giant heart shape of long grass. Spray paint your names inside. Hire a landscape company to cut your bushes into figures and shapes that your partner likes. They can also plant a flower bed that spells out a name or special message. During the winter you can spray a message in the snow with a pump bottle filled with water mixed with food coloring.

36. It is written in the stars. "Star light, Star bright, the first star I see tonight…" is that of my lover's. Have a novelty star named after your partner and dream upon it together. The International Star Registry offers several unique gift package options. $54-$139 1-800-282-3333 – www.starregistry.com

Gift your partner a telescope to open first or have one already set up in some magical romantic place and pre-focused upon "his" star. Then let him unwrap the novelty ownership certificate. Share an evening sipping wine together on a blanket star gazing.

37. Charmed. Enhance your gift; buy your partner a star shaped necklace charm or cuff links so he/she may keep this beautiful gift close to his/her heart. Have the star's name and location engraved on it. If you are on a budget, buy a charm sized wooden star and some necklace rope from your local craft store, drill a small hole for the rope, and using a wood burner, inscribe the name of the star or location number into it. As a gift for my nephew Andrew's Baptism, I named a star in his honor then made him the wooden star-charm chain listed above to hang from his bedroom mirror. While it only cost $2.79 to make, it meant more because of the time, effort, and love that I put into making it.

Birthday & Birth-Day Celebration Ideas

38. Birth-Day. If you are going to celebrate the ultimate gift of life with a child, don't wait a year to celebrate his "first" birthday. Rather than passing out traditional cigars at the hospital, instead, pop open a bottle of Sparkling Cider, pass out birthday hats and birthday cake, and sing "Happy Birth-Day." This way everyone can partake in your celebration. Don't forget to share it with the medical staff that helped deliver your new bundle of joy. Decorate the Birthing Room/incubator with pink or blue Birth-day banners and streamers. My sister and brother-in-law were tearfully joyful when my family marched into the Birthing Room moments after the birth of my nephew - carrying a blazing Birth-day cake while singing Happy Birth-day, with our Birthday hats on.

39. Your hamburger helper. If your significant other just gave birth, help out by making some meals in advance and freezing them. Buy some multi-sized freezer tins and pre-make your meals of lasagna, casseroles, enchiladas, stews, soups, chili, etc. and freeze. When your spouse is tired, sick, up with the baby, or wants a night off from cooking, thaw a meal, toss it into the oven or in a pan on the stove top, dim the lights, play some soft background music, and enjoy an impromptu home-style meal together. It is a simple process: Make a menu or list of your desired meals, gather your recipes, create your grocery list, select your shopping day, begin preparation and pre-cooking work (this is easiest if you do it the night before your cooking day), finally cook, prepare, and stow your meals!

40. The Birthday fairy. My (former) fiancé surprised me at midnight with this sweet and romantic gesture. It is my favorite of many treasured Birthday memories with him. Be the first one to wish your partner a Happy Birthday. Set your vibrating phone or alarm clock to the exact time that your lover was born. If he or she was not born in the wee hours of the night, simply set the alarm for midnight, this way you can still be the first to tell him/her that you are glad he/she was born on his or her birth day. When the clock strikes twelve, reach for your previously hidden goodies from beneath the bed, flip on the lights, jump up on the bed and begin singing "Happy Birthday." Wear a hat, blow a horn, and release some party poppers or birthday streamers. Surround him or her with gifts. To relieve morning breath from your impromptu celebration, share a decorated birthday cupcake or tea cake or simply dispense some nearby breath mints. Enhance the cupcake with a sparkler. Don't forget, the birthday fairy always leaves a gift under the pillow of the birthday honoree to find on his or her special day!

41. Pan-Cake. Try bringing your partner a "Birthday Breakfast" in bed; stack multi-sized pancakes in the shape of a cake and top with a birthday candle or sparkler.

42. Eeny-Meeny-Miny-Mo. For one occasion, my sister was taken to brunch and presented with four sealed envelopes from her husband, in which she was allowed to select just one. Each envelope contained a different prized gift option that remained unknown to her. After much contemplation, she made her selection and opened the sealed envelope…her prize, a shopping spree at the Mall of America and of course the weekend getaway with her husband to Minnesota that accompanied it.

43. Personal growth. Enlist in a new tradition each year on your child's Birthday; decorate the tree that you planted for your child at the time of their birth or paint a new line indicating that he or she is another year older. (Carving into the tree can damage it.)

44. A special delivery for a special delivery. Make an extra special acknowledgement to the mother of your child who made nine months worth of bodily (and some personal) sacrifices. Consider a nice piece of jewelry or a "day of beauty" at the local spa. Make it a point to recognize her each year on your child's Birthday, perhaps you could send her one flower for each year that your child celebrates a Birthday. Consider making her a personalized "Coupon Book." Simply pick and choose your favorite Romance Coupons, awaiting you in the back of this book, cut them out, copy them on fine paper, staple them together, gift wrap, and present them to her.

45. Ten-fold. Acknowledge your wife on your child's birthday with a small token of appreciation gift, wrap it in "Thank you" paper and present on your child's birthday.

46. A penny for your thoughts. Months and months prior to your partner's special day, ask them to write you a "wish" list or casually try and find out a "wish" that he/she has. Wrap up a shinny penny from the year your partner was born and let her know that when she makes a wish as she tosses the coin that her wish is certain to come true. Or, wrap up a single unlit Birthday candle and let your sweetie know that she just received the magic candle, and when she makes a wish as she blows out that candle that you'll put on her cake – her wish will surely come true. Pull out a gift that contains a wish from her list. On one occasion, I lured my (former) significant to the mall so I could fictitiously pick up some alterations. As we passed by the wishing well, I presented him with a small gift and requested that he open it there. It was a lucky penny with similar instructions as above. After he closed his eyes tight, made his wish and tossed the lucky penny into the water, I pulled out an envelope for him to open that contained a map with clues to a certain store location within the mall. There waiting for him at Ticket Master were two tickets to a concert he had been "wishing" to see and a handmade certificate for a night at the adjoining hotel.

Apology: When Saying "I'm Sorry" Just Isn't Enough

47. Da Plane! Da Plane! A Traci Bogan classic! Hire a plane (or be lucky enough to have a friend who owns one and will do you the favor) to circle around your partner's house pulling a banner or sky writing that says "I'm Sorry." Make pre-arrangements with a friend to call and ask your partner to go outside. You will be waiting on bent knee, holding a giant sign that has a big arrow pointing "up." After the plane has gone, turn your sign over to offer the words "Really, Really Sorry." If he or she is still upset with you, then it's time to go and let him or her ponder over the situation, but as you leave, place a single flower on the ground with an attached note requesting that your partner pluck a petal off one by one to the theme of "(s)he loves me - (s)he loves me not" only ask him/her to switch the words to "forgive him/her-forgive him/her not." Make sure that the flower has an odd number of petals on it, so he/she will end with "forgive him/her." This service is offered at a plethora of nationwide locations. 1-877-2-FLY-ADS – www.flysigns.com

48. Brownie points. Maybe you're looking to stay out of the dog house or to win extra brownie points, hire the plane to pull a "Happy Birthday or Anniversary," "John loves Mary," or "Will you marry me?" sign.

49. Olive you. Extend the olive branch…literally! Have an olive branch delivered from halfway around the world with your attached apology, right to the door. Call your local florist and find out how to arrange for this very special order. (Note: Not all florists can accommodate this truly unique request.)

50. Knock, knock! Who's there? Leave your sweetheart speechless by sending him or her a telegram.

51. Balloon-O-Gram: Surprise your sweetie with a bundle of balloons. 1-800-Balloons or 1-800-225-5666 – www.1-800-balloons.com

52. Ole Fashioned Historic Telegram: Send your sweetheart a really special delivery.Western Union Telegrams offers overnight delivery. 1-800-325-6000 – www.westernunion.com

53. The sorcerer's stone. Buy one of those beautiful little stones that say "Forgive" on it. Place the "Magic Stone" in a beautiful tiny box or treasure chest; cradle it atop some crushed gold flakes from your local hobby shop, dried olive branch leaves, or rose petals you've kept from your first date or wedding day. Add a faint whisper of his/her favorite fragrance inside. Wrap this treasure in the most beautiful wrapping paper that you can find. Design a card on parchment paper, burn the edges for an ancient mystical look. The front side of your card will read "This is a Magic Stone. Sometimes the greatest gifts of all come in small packages." The inside of the card will read "One of the greatest authentic powers we each possess is the power of forgiveness. I hope that this Magic Stone encourages you to exercise that power and enjoy the freedom that forgiveness offers to the forgiver and to the forgiven. Please forgive me."

If you want to add a bit of humor to it, on the back of the card write: "And if that doesn't happen anytime soon, maybe in the meantime, we could just make up?"

Turn to stone. If you really screwed up, buy a stone small enough to have made into a necklace charm later on, to be worn as a powerful reminder of the awakening that resulted from this negative experience.

54. Eat your words. Have an "I'm Sorry" cake made at your local bakery, using your partner's favorite flavor cake. Deliver it with a half dozen personalized balloons that will spell out "Really-Really-Sorry-Please-Forgive-Me." Write one word on each balloon and coordinate. Arrive with your portable music maker softly playing "If you leave me now" by Chicago. If that doesn't work, start singing it!

55. Your presents fill the room. If you are at odds with your partner and have missed a holiday, birthday, or special occasion (and are certain that you will eventually reconcile your relationship), buy a gift for your special someone and lovingly hang onto it until the two of you reunite. Let your special someone know that he/she was in your thoughts on that special day. Consider recreating the missed special occasion or celebration.

Some friends of mine had separated a month before the Christmas Season. After a four month break, they reconciled. I gently suggested that he could surprise her by recreating the first Christmas that they had missed in their ten years together. One day she arrived home to a mini gift-bearing tree, a colorful rendition of interior Christmas décor, and a full gamut Turkey dinner. I am told that the look on her face was as priceless as the delayed celebration.

56. Spell it out. Advertise your heartfelt apology by way of renting a marquee or billboard. Use the back window of your car to display your message written with car chalk, or release your "inner-child" and decorate his or her sidewalk using sidewalk chalk.

Ideas for Business Trips or Separate Vacations

57. Sweet surprise. Secretly pack a favorite homemade treat inside your partner's luggage or carry on.

58. Card-nal rule. Slip a perfume or cologne scented card or love note inside of a shirt or pants pocket in his/her suitcase so he/she will find it after his/her arrival when getting dressed. You can also leave a few marked cards or letters to open up on certain days of the week, suggesting to him or her all of the things that you will do for him/her or to him/her when he/she gets home.

59. Love Bytes. If he or she is traveling with a laptop, include a favorite DVD movie or make your own for your partner to find or discreetly change a computer screensaver to your favorite photo of the two of you.

60. Lend a hand. Trace your hand on a piece of paper and in the center of the palm area write the words "Place hand here & hold" or "You'll always have a hand to hold." Add a light spray of his/her favorite fragrance of yours to the paper and mail it or leave it for your partner to find.

61. Picture perfect. Place a photo (current or from when you first began dating) of yourself in the photo sleeve of his/her wallet or proudly carry your partner's photo in yours.

62. Object of my affection. Give your partner a token of your love, leaving him/her with something to look forward to upon his/her return. Surprise your sweetie with these keepsake pewter vouchers: "good for one hug," "good for one kiss," "good for one massage," "good for breakfast in bed," and "good for one roll in the hay." The best part about giving these is you might just get what you want in return. Each set

contains two tokens of each design, and comes in an attractive pouch. www.uncommongoods.com

63. Find your way back. Give a compass ring, necklace, and cufflinks with a note that says "So you will always find your way back to me." www.uncommongoods.com

64. The Missing piece. Let your partner know that he/she is the missing piece in your life. This handcrafted precious set of two sterling silver pendants joins to proclaim "You are the missing piece" when it's put together, but can separate into two necklaces so you and your better half are always linked. Or, surprise him/her by secretly slipping it into your sweetheart's luggage with a note card for him/her to find on the trip. www.uncommongoods.com

65. Tucked away. If you are away from each other, call your partner at his approximate bed time just to say good-night and I love you. If you have time, read him his favorite bed-time story over the phone. Just for fun, consider creating your own story line, using the two of you as the main characters. You can also have one specially designed for you: Get "your story" put in writing for $49.95. www.yourstory.com or "When we first met" is a personalized memory book for $45.00 available at www.whenwefirstmet.com.

66. Operator, give me a line. Talk seductively to your lover on the phone, let him/her feel your presence and touch through the miles between you. Sometimes it is easier to be uninhibited and vulnerable when no one is watching.

67. Panty-less. Ladies wrap your sexiest panties in rose petals or dried miniature roses with a note that says "Forget Me Not" and have that package delivered to your partner's hotel. The hotel will hand carry the package to his room for you. Use the rose petals from the same roses that your partner once gifted you with on some special occasion. Or you can hide your panties in your partner's suitcase for him to find when he unpacks. Or if you are the one staying at the hotel, send your "special delivery" to your partner at home.

68. Sweet dreams. Have your photo inlaid on a pillow (or a full body pillow) and leave it for him or her in the bed when you leaving on a trip! Spray it with your cologne or perfume. Embroider "I Love You" on the pillowcase.

69. Missing you. Contact the hotel where your partner is staying, in advance, and have a chilled bottle of champagne or wine waiting in his/her room when he/she arrives or ask the staff if they can stock the mini-bar specifically with your partner's favorite beverage and snacks. You can also mail a card or send a fax addressed to his/her room number and have it waiting upon check-in. For an extra special surprise, request that room service go into his or her room, prior to arrival and pull down the sheets. But rather than the usual chocolates adorning the pillows, ask that the hotel staff instead ornament the bed using rose petals. Have them spell out your names together inside a heart or write "I miss you." Hotel personnel have always been enthusiastic to accommodate these requests and simply charge your credit card for the roses and beverages. When your sweetheart arrives to his/her suite, he or she will be absolutely stunned!

70. Gram Central. Another one of my favorite things to do is to send a "Shot-O-Gram" or "Drink-O-Gram" to the room or at the lounge. Simply call the hotel/lounge to have a beverage sent over to your sweetheart and pay by credit card right over the phone. I often times send these to my friends around the globe. Just the other day I sent a "Drink-O-Gram" to a friend in Phoenix on her birthday. When she arrived at her favorite watering hole, she was greeted with a birthday drink and message from me.

71. Here with me. My favorite creation. For the ultimate surprise, get there first and lie waiting atop the comfort of satin bed sheets (from home), bearing only a single red rose while encircled in the glow of a hundred tea-candles. To further adulate your affections, fashion an "I Missed U" chocolate syrup creation across your mid-section. Have your favorite sounds of romance whispering in the background. Like I said, really surprise your best friend and lover! Or, emulate this scenario as a "Welcome Home" gift for your partner.

72. R.S.V.P. Prior to your partner's departure, present him or her with a "going away" gift and tell him that it is so he will have something to look forward to when he returns. Give him/her an elegant basket containing massage gels or bath essentials with an "appointment card" attached to be redeemed on his return date. Ask him/her to bring home the "Do Not Disturb" sign.

73. The Pick of the day. On your way home from work, pull the car over and get out to hand pick wild flowers for your sweetheart and tell her how much she drives you "wild." If you are away from each other on a business trip or separate vacation, hand carry a souvenir from the place you were - wild flowers from Montana, a small collection of fall leaves from Maine, a jar of sand from Fiji, or river rocks from that gorgeous bank you saw in Wisconsin. Tell him/her that you thought of him/her the moment you saw these particular items or that the specific place where you found the item was a place that you knew he or she would have loved and that you wanted to share a piece of it.

74. Wild - for you. My friend's husband, while on a "guys' getaway" hunting trip, plucked some beautiful wild flowers from deep within the wilderness, stuck them in a cup of water, on the dashboard and drove them back home some 500 miles to hand deliver them to his wife.

Weddings and Funerals, Proposals, and Anniversaries

75. The butterfly effect. Butterflies are beautiful creatures that have a great deal of symbolic meaning. Indian folklore and legends are filled with references to butterflies; they represent the transformation that occurs when two people unite their lives. Enhance the symbolism surrounding your wedding day by having each one of your guests simultaneously release a butterfly packet. This is an absolutely a breathtaking vision that will never be forgotten. These packets will be delivered to your door one day prior to your special day. Toll Free rush orders at no extra charge!
1-866-359-6265 – www.butterflyreleases.com

76. The Wedding Singer. Surprise your new bride or groom on your wedding night in your new sexy musical panties or Tuxedo underwear. Each bride and groom style plays "The Wedding March." Or, wear them on the night you are going to propose.
www.ebay.com (search for musical underwear)

77. The Genie Grants Three Wishes. Another Traci Bogan original, you are the Genie and you are going to grant your partner 3 wishes. You will give your partner one "wish" at a time for him to place under his pillow at night and it is up to you to bait and switch the "wish" for that of his "granted wish" gift. You can grant your partner's three wishes, three consecutive nights in a row, once a week or once a month for three months, whatever works for you and your budget. Wish three, the grand finale, stands on its own. Feel free to revise the layout to your own liking.

Wish #1. Save the wishbone from a turkey or a whole chicken. (I like the chicken wish bones because they are miniature and cute and fit perfectly in a gold necklace charm sized box, and my local butcher saves them for me.) Clean it off and let it dry out. Wrap the dried wishbone in a nice little box and present it with a card that reads on the front cover "May all of your wishes come true." On the inside of the card, list three wishes. Make sure that all three wishes are something that you know your sweetie wants and you are capable of granting. Tell him or her that he or she is allowed to choose just one wish from the list to have granted by the Genie. Explain in the card, that legend has it that in order for the 1st wish to come true, you and he/she must first break the wish bone together while thinking of the wish. Then ask your partner to circle the one wish of his/her choice and place the wish card and the broken wishbone under the pillow that night. If the wish card and broken wishbone are gone in the morning, the wish is sure to come true. Remove the contents from under the pillow and replace with the "granted wish" gift (like the tooth-fairy) under the pillow for him/her to find in the morning or leave it next to the bed if the "granted wish" gift is large in size. If the "granted wish" needs to be fulfilled outdoors or at another location, still try granting the wish within 24 hours of the wishbone being placed under the pillow.

(The same technique and time frames should apply to wishes two and three as well.)

Wish #2. Go to a garden or field and pluck the fluffy dandelion weed that releases all of the furry flurries when you blow on it (like you may have done you were a kid). Collect one that is in full bloom and cut the stem up to about a quarter in length from the furry head. To secure this "wish" for gift giving, gently place it inside of the slot of a jewelry type box; such as an earring (you will have to take a knife and widen the hole/slot a bit.) or ring box. (These can be easily found at your local jeweler.) Make sure that when you close the box, the top will not rub the fur off of the dandelion head. Because the ring box slot works so perfectly, you can also remove that section from a ring box itself and secure it to different box for fear of misleading or disappointing your partner, who may have had a false hope of receiving a ring from you. The purpose of the "slot" is simply to secure the "wish" so it can be delivered without disruption. Be innovative with your own ideas. Again, wrap up the "wish" and present it with a card that reads on the front cover "May all of your wishes come true." On the inside of the card, list three wishes. Make sure that all three wishes are something that you know your sweetie wants and you are capable of granting. Again choose just one wish from the list to be granted by the Genie. Explain in the card that legend has it that in order for the 2nd wish to come true, your partner must blow the wishes off of the wish head while thinking of the wish. Then ask him or her to circle the one wish of choice and place the wish card and the broken wish head under the pillow that night. If the wish card and broken wish head are gone in the morning, the wish is sure to come true.

Wish #3 Save the best wish for last. Place a shiny penny from the year your love was born in a tiny box (again, the slot of a nice looking velvet ring box is a perfect fit to secure the lucky penny). Wrap it up beautifully and present it to your partner with a card that reads on the front cover "May all of your wishes come true." On the inside of the card, explain that a final wish will be granted by the Genie and legend has it that in order to receive the 3rd wish, he must go and pluck his lucky penny into a magic (fill in the blank) fountain/pond/ lake/river/ creek/ocean at midnight (or whatever time you choose; the time of your first date, etc.). For added fun, enclose a map to this specially selected destination. (Make arrangements with a friend to make certain that your partner is there at the designated time.) If the lucky penny has been tossed by the stroke of (whatever time you select), then a third and final wish of his choice will be granted. Grant his/her biggest and best wish at the wishing well, Prince/Princess Charming! Be romantic and set the scenery to be a fairy tale romance straight out of a book. Wish number three would make for a perfect marriage proposal or pregnancy announcement.

If getting married is what he or she has always dreamed of with you, now is the perfect opportunity to propose. Show that fairy tale wishes really do come true. When he or she arrives at the designated time, be waiting at the fountain in a tuxedo or your finest Prince/Princess Charming clothes, on one knee, surrounded in roses and tea candles, with "your song" playing softly in the background. Arrange the tea candles to spell out your special message in the glow of candles such as "Will You Marry Me?" or "Please Say YES!" (Or, "Baby," "Mother/ Father to be," etc.). If your partner says "yes," make a wish together as you pitch the lucky penny into the magic fountain of youth or eternity. Where I live, tea candles are sold in bags of 100 for $5.99. A picture perfect candle-lit proposal will require between 3-4 bags and the sight of your message lit-up in the dark will be priceless!

Whatever your partner's wish may be, create a scene that bestows tremendous symbolic and magical significance. After all, it is not very often that a Genie comes along and grants anyone three wishes! Make this a memory and a moment that will be forever cherished!

Suggestion: If it is a lady who you are presenting the three wishes to, you can instead substitute one of the above wish options by purchasing the glass diamond shaped bottle of "WISH" perfume by Chopard of Paris. Present this gem gift-wish with a card that reads on the front cover "May all of your wishes come true." On the inside of the card, list three wishes. Make sure that all three wishes are something that you know your sweetie wants and you are capable of granting. Tell her she is allowed to choose just one wish from the list, to have granted by the Genie. Explain to her in the card, that legend has it that in order for her (1st or 2nd) wish to come true, she must first release the power of the wish by spraying one squirt of the WISH perfume onto the wish card while thinking of her desire. Then ask her to circle the one wish of her choice and place the perfume scented wish card under her pillow that night. Again, let her know that if the wish card is gone in the morning, the wish is sure to come true.

You can further substitute one of the wishes by using the donation receipt card from the "Make-A-Wish Foundation®." Wrap up the donation card receipt "wish" and present it with a card that reads on the front cover "May all of your wishes come true." On the inside of the card, list three wishes. Make sure that all three wishes are something that you know your sweetie wants and you are capable of granting. Your partner is allowed to choose just one wish from the list, to have granted by the Genie. Explain that legend has it that "when you give, you get!" Go on to say, that someone has made a donation to the "Make-A-Wish Foundation®" in his or her honor because of his/her dedicated generosity to (a cause/being a good friend/taking care of a child or parent, etc.). Explain that he/she must circle the one wish of his or her choice and place the donation receipt-wish card under the pillow that night. If the wish card is gone in the morning, the wish is sure to come true. Remove the contents from under the pillow and replace with the "granted wish" gift (like the tooth-fairy) under the pillow for him or her to find in the morning or next to the bed if the "granted wish" gift is large in size. If the "granted wish" needs to be fulfilled outdoors or at another location, still try granting the wish within 24 hours of the donation card receipt "wish" being placed under the pillow.

78. I Do, I Do, I Do. Renew your matrimonial vows at 20, 25, 30, or 50 years of marriage. This can be a personal ceremony as if you were eloping, or you can re-create your wedding ceremony and ask your children to stand in as your bride's maids or groomsmen. Go on that honeymoon you never had or take a second honeymoon and book the bridal suite at a fancy hotel. Buy the ring you couldn't afford at the time or up-size the ones that you have or spring for another wedding reception inviting those who bore witness to your special occasion the first time around. Whatever the wildly romantic escapade you choose to renew your love and re-fan those flames, don't forget the "Do Not Disturb" sign!

For Christmas one year, my mother and her two brothers arranged for a surprise vow renewal ceremony for their parents. The pastor came to the house on a snowy Christmas Day and preformed a touching wedding vow renewal as each of their children filled in as bride's maid and groomsmen and "gave the couple away." All the grandchildren filled in as witnesses. It was absolutely heart-warming!

79. Cemented bond. Write your names in the cement of your new patio or walkway and draw a heart around them; be certain to include the date. Create your own personalized stepping stones or handprints using Plaster of Paris design kits found at your local craft store. Be creative, frame your matrimonial handprints on one side of a picture frame and add your wedding photo to the other side.

80. Picture this. Give your partner a truly unique and romantic gift. Have your photo in-laid in gold and laser engraved on items such as tie bars, cuff links, rings, pendants, lockets, and charms. www.giftsongold.com

81. A gift that makes scents. Perfume-Personalized. Fragrances are known to have a strong influence on the human psyche. In just an instant, they can reveal or reinforce memories and arouse our inner most desires. Create the ultimate romantic gesture and treasure with a one-of-a-kind perfume or cologne for your loving bride or groom on your wedding day. Have your wedding scent delivered to your sweetie each year on your anniversary. www.romanceher.com/perfume.htm

82. Eternal honeymoon. Make it a point to tell every new person you meet that you are on your "honeymoon". Men, introduce your lady as your "bride", even if you have been married for twenty years. This "honeymoon" mentality adds the magic spice to keep any marriage from going stale.

83. Tree of life. Plant a tree on your wedding day and watch it grow up as you grow old together. (If you are already married, plant a tree on your anniversary, you can still watch it grow as you continue to grow old together.) Paint your initials in a heart on your tree (carving into the tree can damage it). Plant a tree for each child you bear and watch them both grow together. Bury a time capsule under "your" tree. Instead of having expensive long-stemmed roses delivered to your sweetie that will die in a week, have a baby tree delivered that will likely outlive you both.

84. Up, up, and away. It doesn't get much more romantic than this: Imagine your wedding proposal in a hot air balloon, while being swept off to a romantic bed and breakfast.1-800-SKY-RIDE'S Thrill Planet has partnered with Nationwide Bed & Breakfast providers to offer you a romantic addition to your hot air ballooning experience. Choose from one of Thrill Planet's special packages designed to create an unforgettable moment for your wedding proposal, feed the flames of romance with a special Anniversary Getaway, or have Thrill Planet customize a romantic adventure just for you! 1-800-759-743 – www.ThrillPlanet.com

85. And I thank you. Let your partner know that you would do it all over again. Wrap your anniversary gifts in wedding paper or gift wrapping that says "Thank you" and decorate it with copied photos from your wedding day.

86. My sweetheart. How about giving your partner your whole heart today. Surprise him/her and all of your guests with your "sweetest" romantic idea yet, personalized candy conversation hearts. Indeed, you will be the conversation of the evening! www.bellaregalo.com/trista_ryan_personalized_candy_hearts.html www.mymms.com – www.chocolographyboutique.com

87. Written in stone. Have a brick, stone, or tile laser engraved with your wedding photo, names, or wedding date and grace your garden with it or create a brick path that bears the names of your wedding party or all of your guests if you can spare the expense. Or, use the engraved brick as the visible foundation if you are building your own home. This is a timeless gift.
www.cutinstone.biz – www.royalehouse.com

88. Make a fortune. And share the wealth! Let all of your wedding guests indulge in the good fortune of your special day with your own custom fortune cookies tailored to commemorate your day. www.cookiehq.com (Mention coupon code SAVE 10 and receive 10% discount on regular cookie orders.)

89. The wedding singer. I have two friends who both surprised their bride and groom by singing "their song" or a special song to their partner on their day. One of them even took singing lessons just for the occasion. It was a beautiful and romantic profession of their love.

90. Living Legacy. Create a living memorial where people can go to grieve, share their memories, read about your loved one's life and legacy or simply light an online memorial candle that will forever burn. www.personalizedmemorial.com

91. Ever after. Purchase a joint cemetery plot or mausoleum space. Let your partner know that not only do you want to spend your life with him/her but you also want to spend eternity with him/her. The topic of death is not an easy one for some and making funeral/ burial arrangements after your loved one passes on can be even harder during that difficult time of mourning. Make it easier for your partner and on your partner by pre-planning and securing both your arrangements and final wishes. Plan a special dedication to your partner to be written on his or her stone. Allow him/her to see it so he/she can appreciate your sentiment. This is also a good time to consider writing up a will and discussing each other's final wishes. My grandparents spent 50 years together without ever knowing what the other wanted at their lives' ends. Do you know what your partner's final wishes are? Does he/she know what yours are? Now is a good time to find out.

92. In memory of. If you are joining matrimonial vows and either of you has a deceased parent, go the extra mile and show your thoughtfulness to your partner by including the memory of his/her (or your own) deceased parent(s) in your ceremony. Include the beloved parent(s) framed photo on a mantel and take a moment to honor them by walking up and lighting a candle in their memory or as a gesture of their presence. Another thoughtful and beautiful gesture would be to deliver the bouquet, together, from your wedding day, and place on the deceased parent(s) grave. In this touching story, one bride left two empty chairs adorned with flowers in memory of her grandparents at her outdoor ceremony.

93. The will to live. Let your earthly testimony live ever after. Make a video will or simply make a video of your life to leave behind as a memento for your descendents to treasure and unborn generations of your heritage to one day know a piece of you. A couple days before I departed for my world tour, I sat in front of my tripod for 30 minutes or so, leaving my final words to my loved ones in case I didn't make it home. I secured it in an envelope and gave it to my mother with strict instructions for the package to remain sealed in the safe in case that fateful day arrived.

94. Mourning light. No one loved your sweetheart or pet more than you! Bring comfort and remembrance with a meaningful collection of bereavement and condolence gift ideas to memorialize the memory of your loved one. This Web site is one of my personal favorites. www.thecomfortcompany.net

95. (D)-Fine Art. While this is a controversial sentiment of your undying love, The Eternally Yours Company will mix the cremated remains of your loved one with oil paint and make a one of a kind painting, collage, landscape, or a framed abstract piece of art to ensure that your loved one will always be hanging around. www.memorialart.com

Vacations in your own Backyard

96. Hawaiian Luau in a box. This complete "Luau in a Box" contains a Romantic Luau for 2 adults. A great alternative if you can't afford that dreamy Hawaiian vacation. Bring the essence of the islands right to your front door! A Hawaiian luau is not just a meal, it is an experience! And one that your partner will never forget! All food is shipped frozen/chilled and all you have to do is heat & serve. Price includes shipping and handling in the U.S.A. via FedEx Standard Overnight. www.LuauKing.com (Mention Romance-411 and receive a 10% discount.)

97. Private Oasis. Rent a palm tree! For those living in South Eastern Wisconsin and Illinois, who appreciate the tropical and magnificent palms of the west and south, you can actually rent a live palm tree for the summer! I have a friend in Wisconsin who rents one palm tree to place by his pool side lounge chair at home, making it feel more like a vacation spot, and another one to place outside of the windows at his restaurant, to enhance the scenery for his patrons. Palm tree rentals in Wisconsin cost around $200, and they deliver and pick up at summer's end when it is time for the palm to "head south" and be tucked in for the winter. Have the palms of the tropics transported right into your backyard! "The Tropics" located in Racine, Wisconsin. 262-637-4140.

98. Nuts for you. Is all this tropical bliss still out of your budget? Fear not! You can still bring the tropics right inside of your home with an Island Sprouting Coconut. Plant or float your own Coconut palm that sprouts right from the coconut itself! The sprouting coconut makes a great house plant for years. This tropical and romantic gift is shipped to your home directly from Hawaii for only $45.99, including shipping and easy to use instructions. They also ship fresh Hawaiian Leis and a large assortment of other Island goodies. www.hawaiiangoodies.net

99. Smore fun. Pitch a tent, build a mini bonfire, roast marshmallows, and dream beneath the stars together in your own backyard.

Other Vacation Ideas:

100. Tunnel of Love. You don't have to travel to Venice for this experience, but you will feel as if you are there! Transport yourself in time to Newport Beach, California, Irving, Texas, Lake Las Vegas, Nevada, Myrtle Beach, South Carolina, and Orlando, Florida for an authentic gondola ride. This is romance at its finest. Create an impression and a memory with that special someone as a charming gondolier silently glides you through quaint canals. Complete your romantic adventure with champagne, fine chocolates, soft music, and gourmet meals served on crystal, silver, and china. www.gondola.com (With links to other gondola service locations.)

Gondola services: You can send an intriguing and romantic "Message in a Bottle" during your cruise. The gondolier will inconspicuously place the bottle in the water. Your loved one will then be asked to retrieve it as it "poses a navigational hazard". This is where curiosity will pique the recipient's interest as to what's inside and slowly, as your sweetheart unravels the scroll, your pre-personalized message will touch his or her heart. Gondola Adventures, Inc. will transfer your special message over to parchment scroll paper using "Calligraphy Style" font. The scroll is then rolled, tied with ribbon and placed in a clean, glass bottle which has been decorated for the occasion. 1-877-4-GONDOLA – Email: nevada@gondola.com

101. Play mate. Charter a romantic sunset cruise or dinner cruise.

102. Wine Not? Spend a weekend at a winery-resort or experience a wine tasting in Napa Valley, offering a variety of tours by bus, van, limousine, train, carriage, hot air balloons, and helicopter. Take off on a quiet kayaking tour or spend time together making your way across Sonoma. Some may wish to explore the wineries with tours by bicycle. Stop for a picnic after winery tours in an open carriage pulled by a matched pair of horses or, experience the nostalgia of an antique limousine convertible the way the movie stars of the 1940's did when they arrived in Napa and Sonoma for romantic getaways! www.napawinetours.net

103. Divine wine. Have your own personalized wine delivered to your home each month; join a wine club or wine of the month club.

104. Private label party. Surprise your partner with an exclusive in-house or outdoor wine tasting. Have your name or logo labeled or etched on your wine (or beer) bottles. Personalized private label wines are the perfect wine gift for any occasion. They also make unforgettable corporate gifts or promotional items. www.signaturewines.com – www.winegiftclub.com

Lending a Helping Hand Together

105. Give the gift of life. As a symbol of your commitment to sharing your lives, become an organ donor, donate blood or plasma, or get on the bone marrow registry. Donate in memory of, or in dedication to a loved one. Perhaps you can gift your milestone-donation card to him/her as a token of your support to the cause or the cure. Make a financial contribution to your loved one's favorite charity, wrap your gift receipt or check carbon as a gift for him or her.

106. Save a life. Rescue an animal from your local shelter or Humane Society and present it to your partner with a big red bow around its neck. If you do not want the responsibility of a pet, can't have one, or are allergic, you can still help. Donate to your local Humane Society or support your local zoo by adopting an animal there. If you're not an animal lover, then adopt a tree or a highway.

107. Pitching in. Volunteer together.

Time for the Two of Us

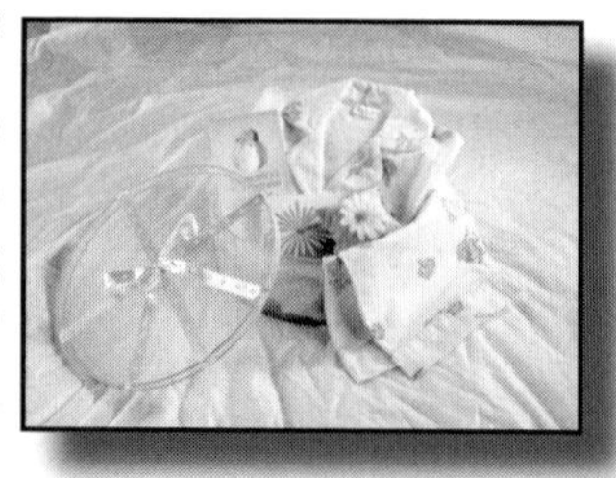

108. A Pajama Gram. A slumber party for two! If you want to give a gift that really spoils someone, send them a PajamaGram. They'll receive the softest, most luxurious pajamas, along with a gift card, lavender sachet, and a "Do Not Disturb" sign for the door, all delivered in a keepsake organza hat box. Your PajamaGram Pajamas can be ordered by 5 p.m. EST and are guaranteed for overnight delivery. What a great way spend the day together, lounging in your pajamas! 1 -800-GIVE-PJS – www.PajamaGram.com

109. Date night. Make an investment of quality time with your sweetheart. Set up a weekly or monthly payment plan to each other. The anticipated outcome of your collaborated "interest" to this investment should prove very rewarding. Dedicate your time with your partner or your family by committing to a weekly/monthly tradition. Maybe it is Sunday brunch, followed by a nice afternoon drive, taking in the views of a different park, country road, or pie or malt shop each time. Perhaps it is an hour of sharing pastries and coffee over the Sunday morning newspaper or just planning for the upcoming week. Maybe it's a day of child-like play: throwing a Frisbee around on a sun-kissed beach, playing catch or badminton in your own backyard, going to an amusement park, swinging on the swings at the community park, wrestling around together in the crispy earth-toned fall leaves, or exploring the scenery of a new hiking trail. Hopefully this weekly or monthly commitment will be dedicated to quality "alone" time for just the two of you.

110. Your "Stay-in" power. Hire a sitter to take the kids "out" for the day while the two of you stay "in".

111. Do it anyway day. Surely there are things that your sweetheart likes to do that you don't; give your honey his/her way and enjoy seeing the smile you brought to his/her face.

112. Schmoozing instead of snoozing. Stay in bed snuggling for an extra 15 minutes on a hectic week day morning rather than hitting the snooze button.

113. "Brownie" points. Setting the alarm clock a little earlier than normal and start the morning with pastries and tea together.

114. Rx for a happy relationship. Meet at lunchtime for a picnic in the park or brown bag it in the break room or outdoors on a nearby patch of grass.

115. "Labor" of love. Not all romantic jewelry has to be expensive; here is one working man's way to romance... My uncle worked as a machinist in a factory for many years. When the factory was scheduled to close its doors, he ran his final piece from his last job; it was an intricately cut thumb-sized metal cylinder, a piece that he had run many times over the years. He secured it on a thin piece of hemp rope and brought this jewel home for my aunt as a symbolic token of all his blood, seat, and years...his years of labor, his years of putting food on the table, and his years dedicated to giving her the kind of life of which she had always dreamed.

116. A Super Bowl. If your sweetie is a big sports fan, make him up a super bowl for the Super Bowl. Stuff this neat treat gift-basket with paraphernalia that boasts his favorite team. Top it off with a six-pack of his favorite beverage, favorite tobacco product or gum and a coupon for when he returns home. (You fill in the blank.)

117. You, Me, We. A neat way to decide on your playful or passionate "time-out" interludes is to take turns planning one. I personally like the "you" plan, "I" plan, and "we" plan concept. Give it a try and see the interior mill work of your relationship instantly improve and strengthen.

118. Heat of the moment. Put this book down right now and go give your partner a deep passionate kiss for no reason. Tell him/her something that you appreciate about him or her. Stop reading! Go and do it! Put this book down right now and go give your partner a deep passionate kiss for no reason. Tell him/her something that you appreciate about him or her. Stop reading! Go and do it! Put this book down right now and go give your partner a deep passionate kiss for no reason. Tell him/her something that you appreciate about him or her. Stop reading! Go and do it! I hope you really did it!

119. Memory lane. Go for an after dinner walk or a drive to the place where you first met, proposed, made love, conceived your child, or got married. Share some dessert there instead of at the restaurant. When you get home, carry your lover over the threshold as you did on your blissful wedding day.

120. A shot of Vitamin-C. If you really want your relationship to grow, enlist you and your partner into Sgt. Traci's Boot Camp and reap the rewards for months to come.
www.OperationRomance.com (Mention this ad and save $50!)

121. Too close for comfort. Sit next to each other at the restaurant rather than across from each other.

122. I dig you. Even years after you are married or together, dig up and then wrap up your old high school or college ring and put it on a chain and give it to your partner. Similarly, dust off your old letter jacket and offer it to him/her to wear.

123. Lover's Lane. Take him or her "necking" at that old drive-in location or secret spot you used to frequent together. Dust off your old photos from "back in the days" and reminisce together at your secret spot.

124. At the hop. Recreate your prom with just the two of you.

125. Block Buster love. Drop off a shoulder-strap-style carrying cooler bag at your partner's place of employment packed with both of your favorite cold beverages, a frozen pizza, and a Block Buster gift card with a note requesting a date. Take the extra step and fill a wicker type basket with theater style candy and popcorn packets and bring it out at the start of the movie. Dim the lights and snuggle on the couch. Steal a kiss at intermission.

126. Reel love. Surprise a partner by having someone deliver theater or movie tickets to him or her at work. Where I live, they have a live pianist performing at the front of the movie theater prior to the show's viewing; take advantage of such opportunity by requesting "your" song. If you are not shy about sharing public affection, take the hand of your lover and spontaneously slow dance in the dimly lighted theater or simply hold hands in silence and appreciate the meaning behind the song, that only the two of you share.

127. Reeling in the years. Another romantic idea regarding movies that your partner may really appreciate is to take his/her old home movie reels or VHS tapes and have them made into a DVD movie. This is a sure way to preserve his/her lifetime of memories for a lifetime. Pull out the popcorn and soda and reminisce on days gone by.

128. Where art thou, Romeo? Ring the doorbell, stand below the window or climb up a ladder to recite a love-letter, sing "your song," or quote favorite poetry. This is all the more romantic if you are living together. Be crazy in love tonight, like you were when you first met.

129. First date^2. On one occasion, my (former) fiancé and I had a dinner "date" planned; he sneaked a change of clothes to work and arrived at our home sharply on time, rang the doorbell, with a bouquet of flowers and "picked me up" at our front door for our date. Afterwards, he pulled up in front of our house (rather than parking in the garage as we usually did and going in through the back door) and walked me to our front door, gave me a sweet little kiss, and then asked me if he could come in and spend the night with me.

130. Playing footsie. When your partner arrives home after a long day, greet him or her at the door with his or her favorite beverage. Lead your partner into the living room for a salt-water foot bath. Remove his/her shoes, peel off socks or panty hose, cuff pant legs and gently insert each foot into an ever so soothing foot bath. Caress them, massage them, and love them tenderly. Gently pat them dry and then share some wine and sushi or Chinese food. Don't forget to add rose petals to the foot bath and use them to aid in the foot massage.

131. The Letter. Gather your old love-letters or poems that your partner or you have written through the years and create a "Book of Love" to present at a later time. Show your sweetie how much those letters meant to you to have kept them through the years. Have them professionally bound or pick a favorite and frame it.

132. I wood love you forever. Hand craft a gift for your partner. I created a "wooden" book. It contained thin ring bound wooden pages, each side exposing hundreds of hours of hand-burned inscriptions of love-letters and poems that I had scribed for my (former) fiancé. It was intended to be the ultimate "Book of Love" given on our ultimate day…that was never to come.

133. Carnival love. Pick your partner up for a date and head to the carnival or circus. Ride the Ferris wheel and kiss...mid-air. Share cotton candy, candied apples, and win her a prize. Find the fortune teller and have this soothsayer do a reading for you and your partner together. The fortune teller will read the personalized "good fortune" that you had composed and delivered to him or her earlier that day.

134. Bottoms up. Place a "special request" in her panty drawer, or better yet, replace all the boring old underclothes with sexy new ones. Silk, satin, leather, or lace.

135. Read all about it. Get up early and surprise your partner with his favorite breakfast in bed. Your special delivery should include a copy of the morning newspaper, a tea candle, a single flower, and an additionally nice touch is to serve freshly squeezed juice and a daily supply of multi-vitamins. Perhaps this particular morning edition of the paper will have a special feature inside making an announcement or dedication to your partner.

136. Caring for Colds. If your sweetheart is sick, take the day off of work and nurse him/her back to health; keep your sweetie hydrated with fluids such as water, 100% juice, or hot tea with honey or lemon. Remedy with some home-cooked soup and Jell-O. Pick up his or her favorite movie rental or a couple magazines. If he/she has "the chills," warm his/her socks, slippers, robe, or blanket in the dryer or get a heating pad. Fill a tray table with essentials pertinent to the aliment like Kleenex, Vicks, throat lozenges, vitamins, and cold/flu tabs. Or, offer a gentle back or foot rub or a cool bath to reduce his/her fever or use the "Ease a Cold" bath recipe found on page 103.

137. Bear with me. Send your under-the-weather partner a Bear-Gram! Yes, it's true, misery loves company. This is a thoughtful way to put a smile on your partner's face and show him/her that you are thinking of him/her. These Bears are made in America and guaranteed for life so they'll be loved forever. Each Bear-Gram gift includes a customized handcrafted teddy bear with a personalized greeting card and a candy treat, all packaged in a colorful gift box with an air hole so the bear can breathe. Nothing shows you care like sending a bear! 1 -800-829-BEAR – www.VermontTeddyBear.com

15" Get Better Bear

15" Angel Bear

15" Nurse Bear

138. One Wish. Everyone wishes for something. Make one of your partner's wishes come true.

Seasonal Ideas

139. Frozen moment. Rather than having a snowman grace your front yard at Christmas, have a personalized life-sized ice sculpture created and have it delivered directly to your front yard. Imagine arriving home to the sight of an ice prince drawn to his knee, kissing the hand of his fair lady, or adorning her presence with a sparkling ring box. Some ice sculptors are available for hire to come right to your home and carve their show for you live. If not the beautifully romantic gesture alone, the sight itself is sure to grace the pages of your local newspaper!

140. Guardian Angel. Make a snow angel in your front yard and leave a note aside your bed for your partner to find, telling him that he has a "guardian angel" watching over him. Let him discover his "angel" in the snow. To give it an angelic glow, mix about 10 drops or so of food coloring into a pitcher of ice water (crushed ice works best) and then spread it evenly inside of your angel impression.

141. Melt my heart. During those snowy winter days, take an extra few minutes to clean off your partner's car and warm it up for her. If you happen to pass by her place of employment prior to her finishing the work day, find her car in the parking lot and scrape off the snow and ice from the windows. You can also offer this gesture in the form of a "romance" coupon.

142. Walking in a winter wonderland. Pack a thermos full of hot coffee, tea, or chocolate and take him or her into winter wonderland.

Pull her on a sled through a flurry snow field or double up on one and go down the hill together. When is the last time you made a snowman or snow angels together, had a snowball fight, went ice skating or fishing, made real snow cones, sipped hot chocolate with marshmallows, took a horse-drawn carriage ride or just walked hand in hand between the snow flakes admiring Christmas lights?

143. Memory tree. A great romantic idea for Christmas (or anytime) would be to surprise your partner with a tabletop mini "memory" tree. Secretly collect a tree ornament from every special place that the two of you visited throughout the year. Look forward to adding to it each year. When I was backpacking around the world, my mother requested a tree ornament from every place I visited. I mailed souvenir packages home periodically. I assumed they would eventually be shuffled in with her smorgasbord of ornaments for the Christmas tree the next holiday season; I returned home to find that my mother had a miniature sized "International tree" waiting for me...made with loving thoughts from missing me.

144. Let it snow! Let it snow! Let it snow! After having spent nearly a decade living in the Hawaiian Islands, I can truly appreciate the excitement of the season's first snowfall lightly blanketing the rest of the country. There were some years that slipped by in the islands when it hardly seemed or felt like Christmas to me at all in that wonderful tropical weather. Just think about the look on your partner's face as she awakes to a yard filled with snow on what would have otherwise been a snow-less Christmas. Imagine being the only home on your block to have anything from a light dusting to a heavy blizzard of white winter wonderland snow in the yard. How romantic it would be to make snow angels together, build a snowman, and perhaps, toss a snowball or two? Even on a hot summer's night, you can celebrate the "halfway to Christmas" mark. An affordable option is to rent a blizzard machine, available at many local rental shops or purchase your own online or on e-Bay for a few hundred dollars. They are easy to use and will create an absolutely unforgettable memory! Keywords: snow maker, snow machine, or fake snow. www.rjnworld.com

145. Miracle on ___ Street. If Saint Nick can spare the expense, you can really surprise your sweetheart by having a truck load of real or fake snow dumped directly into your yard. One of my favorite romantic ideas that I have not yet been able to implement.

146. Burning love. Build a roaring fire in the snow and watch its flames twist into the winter winds, abducting lone snowflakes, one by one. Share a blanket/sleeping bag with your lover, while sipping hot chocolate, taking in the beauty of the moment with fire and ice and neighboring Christmas lights.

147. Thanks for giving. Make a special acknowledgement to your partner at Thanksgiving time. Let him or her know how thankful you are that he/she is in your life and for all he/she has done for you. Leave a special gift as an expression of that gratitude next to the pumpkin pie. Perhaps it is the wrapped up wishbone from last year…granting him or her anything he or she may have wished for.

148. You light up my life. Carve a special message on a pumpkin and surprise your partner with it as it glows. One unique idea is to use pumpkins to propose marriage. Create a candlelit path of illuminated carved pumpkins that spelled out "___ Will You Marry Me?" - When your special someone enters the room or arrives to the location, be ready waiting on bent knee. An appropriate Halloween costume for the occasion would be: A Knight in Shining Armor.

149. "Row, row, row your boat. Gently down the stream. Merrily, merrily, merrily, merrily, life is but a dream." Indeed, life is but a dream and it will disappear just as quickly as it came. Don't waste another moment of a beautiful day; pack a romantic picnic, rent a row boat and paddle your lover off to some deserted place for the day. Clear an impression in the tall grass and spread out your blanket to enjoy a nice picnic on fine china or paper plates while sipping wine. Don't forget your bug spray and to leave with everything that you arrived with! Another romantic gesture is to secretly pack your sweetie a light jacket in case it gets chilly and an umbrella in case it rains.

Here are some picnic items to consider:

- Bottle of Wine or favorite beverage
- Cheese and crackers

- Fruit
- Bagels and cream cheese
- Chicken
- Sandwiches/Sub sandwiches (packed in ice)
- Blanket

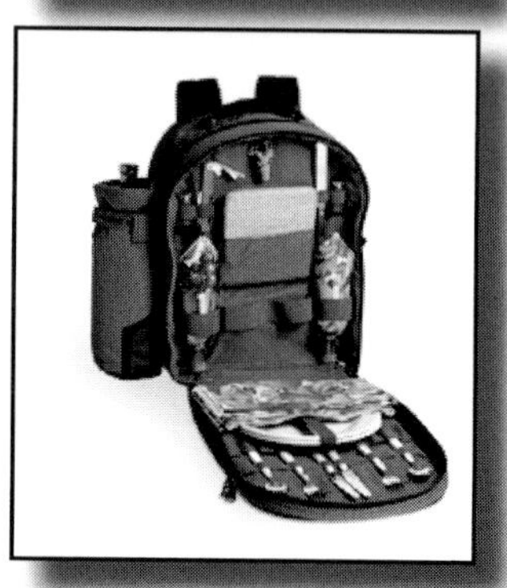

- Kite
- Music/soft/meaningful/romantic
- Book/poem
- Bag for trash
- Bug spray

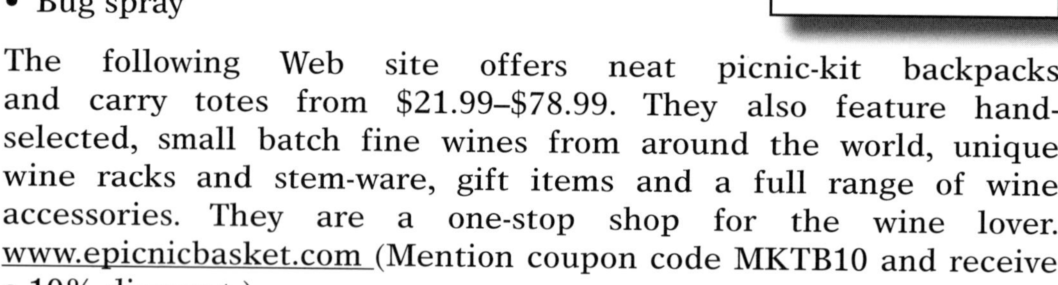

The following Web site offers neat picnic-kit backpacks and carry totes from $21.99–$78.99. They also feature hand-selected, small batch fine wines from around the world, unique wine racks and stem-ware, gift items and a full range of wine accessories. They are a one-stop shop for the wine lover. www.epicnicbasket.com (Mention coupon code MKTB10 and receive a 10% discount.)

150. Waves of music. Once, on a romantic picnic in Hawaii, I had arranged for a friend to pay an unsuspecting visit to our secret seashore location and surprise my guest with a few songs strummed from his acoustic guitar.

151. Horse play. As lovers of horses, a friend of mine took his wife horseback riding for her birthday; he prearranged for the stable personnel to "randomly" choose a horse for his bride, one resembling one she had always wanted and admired. They rode distant trails that eventually lead to a secluded romantic picnic with a giant sign that revealed this message:

"Happy Birthday to the one who has changed my life's course,
I love you as much as you'll love your new horse."

152. Flying high. Send a basket to your partner at work, packed with a kite, sunscreen, sun glasses, a visor or a new hat, and a bottle of wine. Enclose an invitation that requests his presence at such and such place at such and such time and leave a crayon drawn map. When he arrives, have an area already set up for you to relax and enjoy your time together. Make arrangements with his employer to leave work early that day. Stay long enough to watch the sunset. You can also make a nice treasure hunt from this.

Sensual Ideas

Remember, there is nothing shameful in either the beauty of love or how it is expressed. This section is intended to be intimate and sensual, not sexual.

153. Apple of my eye. Recreate the steamy food teasing scene from the movie 9½ weeks. Wear something sexy, blindfold your partner with a silk or satin scarf, and seduce him with a variety of succulent food samplings. Tantalize him using your mouth, fingers, and hands. Allow him or her to cleanse his/her palate in-between food samplings by transferring champagne from your mouth into his/hers. Enhance this sensual experience by adding pudding, fondue, and sponge cake to your arsenal of sweet, wet, and luscious fruits, and decadent foods.

154. An intimate moment. Bathe your lover. To feel the vulnerability of being bathed is truly a pure and intimate experience. There is an art to bathing someone that reaches surfaces far deeper than skin. Bathing your lover is not only sensuous, it is the pinnacle of what intimacy is.

155. Hairs to you. Step outside of your comfort zone and try something that you normally wouldn't. Shave your lover's name or initials into your pubic region or shave your name in his or hers. Make a template by carving your design into a thin piece of cardboard with a razor knife. There are two ways to create your design: The first is by cutting off the surrounding hair around your template. The second is by pulling your hair through the template so only the design impression itself will be nude. Place your template where you want it, press firmly against your skin, and with a headless, electric hair trimmer, trim hair away. Then with a finer and smaller-sized electric razor, smooth, clean, and fine tune your creation. Remember, it's only hair, it will grow back.

156. Hair today, gone tomorrow. Try shaving each other's pubic region for a more erotic feel. Be creative: design a heart, lightning bolt, or the symbol representing a hug or a kiss. Fashion a "landing strip" or simply shave it clean.

157. Dyeing to please you. Be unusually whimsical! Dye your pubic hair your lover's favorite color and then add his or her initials atop that. Use extreme caution when using any hair-dyeing products and read the instructions carefully.

158. Splish splash. Shave the legs of your wife or significant other as she bathes. Later, offer to paint her nails. Treat your husband or lover to a good ol' fashioned lather and straight-edged shave, perhaps out on the back porch some Sunday morning. Do mini home-spa treatments on each other.

159. Sweet everythings. Eat dessert from your lover's nude body using only your mouth. Let him or her do it to you.

160. Because I love you. When you partner arrives home after a long day, greet him at the door and secure a blindfold around his eyes and lead him up to the bedroom. Instruct him not to speak or touch you. Undress him and pamper him with nothing in return.

161. Sensually yours. Release your sensual alter-ego. Try couples yoga or tantric yoga. Consider taking an erotic dance class; learn to belly dance or learn the craft of a temptress, seductress, or pole dancer. Consider taking a strip-tease lesson and perform your own private show for your lover. Be vulnerable.

162. Awakening. Learn about the 5,000 year old Indian tradition of Tantric loving and sexuality. It is truly a sensual and even erotic experience.
www.awakeningshakti.com

Or, visit a Tantric yoga oasis, located in the beautiful Maui, Hawaii.
www.kahuainstitute.com

163. Fantacy island. Your day...your way! Grant your lover a daring fantacy of his or her choice.

164. All the right moves. Sheila Kelley's S Factor is a sensual workout inspired by yoga, Pilates, strip moves, and pole dancing that liberates and empowers women to get in touch with their inner sexuality. The movement is designed to help women appreciate and enjoy the luscious, female curves with which they were born and to free them to move in a powerful, sexy way. To feel proud and happy with yourself is what sexy is! S Factor movement feeds not only your body, but your heart, soul, and mind. www.sfactor.com

Tips for at-home dancing: (By Sgt. Traci)

- Set the stage and music.
- Remain silent.
- Use your index finger to motion your partner towards entering your newly created V.I.P. room.
- Sit him down and hand him a card explaining the ground rules:
- No touching the dancer, only the dancer can do the touching, and no talking.
- Let the show begin. Use a chair...and have an affair with the chair!

Tips for a good at-home stage show: (By Sgt. Traci)

- A black-light light bulb
- A leg garter for ladies
- A furry boa for gals, a loosened neck/bow tie for men & wrist cuffs
- Gloves that slide up your forearm, for ladies
- Stiletto heels for ladies
- A sexy appealing outfit such as satin, leather, or lace
- Glitter lotion and your best perfume for the ladies
- Body oil and great scented cologne for the men

165. Got game? Add some spark and pizzazz to the bedroom; as a couple, visit an Adult Toy-Store and choose some fun bedroom items together, or decide to each pick out something for the other and make it a surprise. Adult board games are also a fun way to add sizzle and anticipation to an intimate evening. www.timefortwo.com

166. Girl's night. Ladies, have a "girl's night" in with your newly found alter-ego, share the wealth with your best girlfriends; host a "Surprise Party" right in your home. A representative from your area will come to your home and display an array of intimate lingerie, sexual enhancement items, and informative books and bedroom "helpers." When each person is ready to order, it will be done privately, confidentially, and discretely. A friend of mine hosted one and actually turned it into a "couples" party, where the men got to privately make the selections for their ladies. To find a representative in your state (and Canada): 1-800-952-1786 – www.surpriseparties.com

167. Barely there. Go skinny dipping together or play naked Twister.

168. Trading places. Wrap a gift for your partner that you will wear.

169. Kneading you. Buy your partner a gift certificate for a massage or take a massage class together. As a seasoned massage connoisseur, there is no massage, in my opinion that is more sensual and intimate than a Thai Massage! I didn't leave Thailand without first getting my certification!
www.learn-massage-online.com
www.peacefulmind.com

Or, pick up a copy of "Erotic Massage: The Tantric Touch of Love" by Kenneth Ray Stubbs.

170. The sound of silence. In total silence, stand toe to toe with your partner and lovingly stare into each others eyes for five solid minutes. This act of raw nakedness is true nourishment for the soul and is equally rewarding as it is difficult to ensue - adding a whole new dimension of truth, communication, vulnerability, and intimacy to your relationship.

171. Moment of truth. Sit across from your partner with your knees touching and while holding hands, look into each others eyes and spend five minutes updating each others wants, needs, and changes. Ask each other how you can better love one another. Really honor, respect, appreciate, and listen to your partner's innermost desires.

Special Delivery or Unique Gift Ideas

172. Send a lobster Gram. This idea is a favorite of mine! I definitely give it two claws up! This is the perfect gift for the lobster purist. Sweet, succulent live Maine lobsters will tantalize the taste buds while the accessories make enjoying this classic feast a snap. It's Lobster Gram's namesake package and is still one of their top-sellers after all these years. There are simply no fresher lobsters available, unless you catch them yourself. Deluxe packages also include the cooking pot, butter warmer, and candle and holder. Choose your menu from a variety of meal packages, offering delivery/same day and next day. 1-800-548-3562 – www.lobstergram.com

173. My sweetie. Express your sentiments creatively through cookie bouquets and gourmet cookie gifts; a perfect way to send your sweet sentiments whatever the reason or season. Whether you're celebrating a birthday, anniversary, the arrival of a new baby, or just want to tell that special someone how much you care. The cookie consultants are happy to assist you in creating just the right gift for your special someone.
1 -888-882-6654 – www.cookiesbydesign.com

174. You float my boat. Try a special delivery by paper boat! Because I love paper boats so much, I am including instructions for you on how to make your own. Start with a love-letter or the newspaper bearing your wedding photos or your child's birth announcement and put a little gift in it - necklace, friendship ring, promise ring, key to your heart or your home. Float it on over to your sweetheart in the bath tub or leave it in a puddle outside the back door for him to find when he arrives home from work.

1. Take a sheet of A4 paper and fold it in half from top to bottom.

2. Fold it in half the opposite way and open out again.

3. Fold the corners to the middle matching the edges to the crease.

4. Fold the spare paper up, turn over and do the same to the other bottom edge.

5. Fold the spare paper up, turn over and do the same to the other bottom edge.

6. Open out from the middle and flatten the opposite way. Tuck the little flaps inside each other.

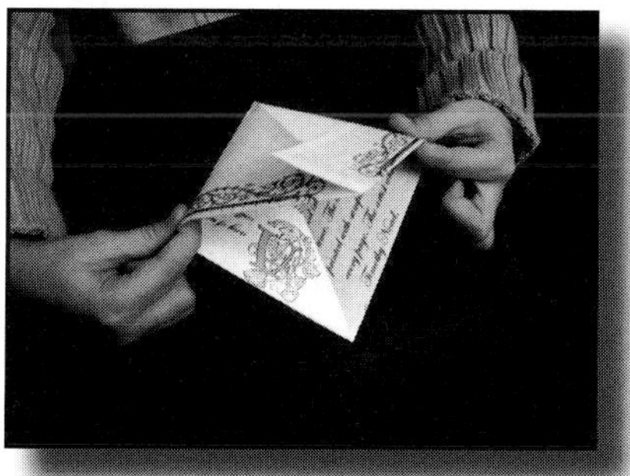

7. Open out from the middle and flatten the opposite way. Tuck the little flaps inside each other.

8. With the open edge towards you, fold the bottom point to the top. Turn over and do the same the other side.

9. With the open edge towards you, pull apart the top folds of paper as far as they will go. Open out from the middle and flatten the opposite way.

10. With the open edge towards you, pull apart the top folds of paper as far as they will go.

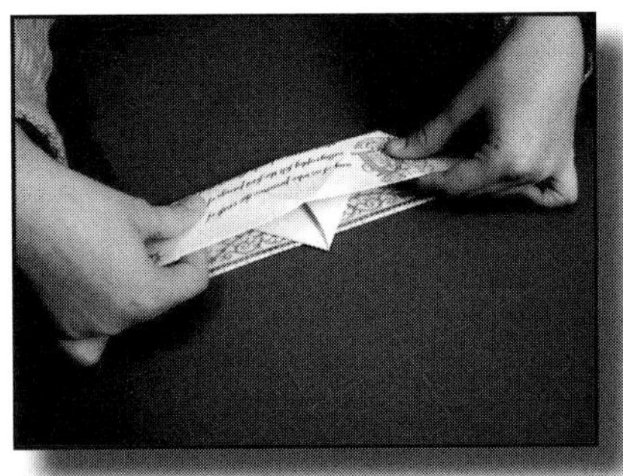

11. Decorate and float! And don't forget to place a little gift inside!

A special thank you to Maria Victoria Garrido for sharing her talent of paper boat making and to her granddaughters, who filled in as guest "hand" models:

Carolina Antonini (9 years old) and Macarena Antonini (12 years old)

175. Sowing the seeds of love. Fe Fi Fo Fum…all you need is water and sun! Give your partner a mysterious magic bean straight out of the nursery rhyme Jack and the Beanstalk. Let your partner grow his/her very own "Magic Bean" to reveal an ingrained secret message that says "I love you" right on the bean itself! Each bean comes in a beautiful velour sachet of "Magic Bean Wishes." The variety will suit each of your celebratory needs: Love, Spiritual, Success, Encouragement, Wedding, Birthday, Baby, Friendship, Sympathy, Family, Get Well, Teacher, etc. These elegant looking sachets are filled with a variety of ten "Magic Bean Wishes" with sayings such as: Forever, Friend, Love, Commitment, Forgive, Baby, I Miss You, Listen, Heal, Create, Talk, etc. There is no extra charge for personalized orders. For this great gift option
www.magicbeanwishes.com

176. Sprouting love. A unique idea for a marriage proposal would be to secure an engagement ring around a magic bean that says "Will You Marry Me?" then wait for the big question to emerge from the soil.

177. Finding Cinderella. The Prince has found a glass slipper and is searching and searching for its rightful owner. Find your Cinderella and return this beautiful 24% Lead Crystal slipper to her now. This elegant gift is sure to capture her heart. Nestled with care in the inside of the shoe is a satin bow with an elegant card that says:

"I have found this Glass Slipper."
"I know it must belong to someone remarkable, someone beautiful and someone I truly love. It must belong to you."
Love, Your Prince Charming.

www.onepassionplace.com (Click on Romantic Gifts.)

178. Pocket full of Posey. Let your feelings "ring" in; buy your partner a Posey ring or Posey pendant. Posey rings are engraved with poetry or romantic sentiments. They can be traced back to classical times but were most popular in the 16th and 17th centuries as wedding rings

and as tokens of love or affection. Couples engraved birthstone rings are also great gifts of sentiment.
www.me2you.com
www.limogesjewelry.com

(Use coupon code SHIPRMC, for Free shipping on entire order from Limoges, one use per customer.)

179. All in one. Another neat idea regarding jewelry that my mother thought of as she was contemplating how she was going to ever wear all the jewelry she had collected or was willed from deceased loved ones through the years, was to have them all melted and designed into one neat piece of wearable jewelry. Now, all of her family treasures and lifetime memories will always be "together" hanging close to her heart in a truly one of a kind family heirloom.

180. Hand-delivery. Ladies, give a "promise" or engagement ring to your man! My sister brought her boyfriend (now husband) a "promise" ring (a Tiffany's mesh band). He wore it on his right ring finger throughout their relationship. When they got engaged, he referred to the "promise" ring as his "engagement" ring. When my sister suggested that they go wedding band shopping, he wanted the promise ring to be his wedding band, so on their wedding day, my sister placed her "promise" of eternal love onto the ring finger of his left hand.

181. Get personal. Let your roses speak volumes by having personal messages embossed in gold. Write a message of up to 30 characters on every rose. This amazing process won't shorten the life of the roses or make them wilt. It is stunningly beautiful!

www.personalcreations.com (Click on specialty shops/personalized flowers.)

182. Get even more personal. Don't just send flowers, everyone does that. Personalize your floral arrangement. Drop off your goodies at the florist; they will include them in the arrangement. Include things like a small bottle of your partner's favorite fragrance, theater or Broadway tickets, a massage certificate, a magazine subscription, or an envelope inside containing airline tickets for two with a photo of your intended destination. If you can't afford that luxury getaway right now, include a love note with a picture of the place that you long to take him or her one day. List one action that you have taken to bring that dream one step closer to reality. I am sure he or she will appreciate the thought of "future" intent together.

183. Visual effects. Deliver a wrapped outfit to her at work with a note attached that says "I can't wait to see you in this tonight."

184. The Masterpiece. Have your lover's portrait painted in oils and present it as a gift. Have a nude or sensual painting made of him or her to grace the private walls of your sleeping oasis. I admire the sensuous explicit art work of Jim Warren. He will paint your one-of-a-kind idea or simply duplicate your favorite existing piece, replacing it with the face of your lover. He can additionally personalize your piece with jewelry and personal inscriptions written in the sand.
www.jimwarren.com

185. The canvas of your life. Have your favorite photograph turned into an oil painting. Imagine magnificent artwork from your photographs. Have a professional artist turn them into beautiful handmade paintings and drawings. Choose from pencil sketches, watercolors, oil on canvas paintings, pastel drawings, and other types of visual arts.

This company did an outstanding job on a rendition of my nephew for his first birthday.

www.canvasartists.com

186. All together now. Have a mosaic photo of your partner or of you & your partner made from the photos of all of your years & adventures together. Create your own "The story of us" in one picture perfect portrait. (250) 477-1812 – www.magicmosaics.com (Mention coupon code MM161 and receive a 10% discount.)

187. A thousand words. Get personal with a new generation of mosaic art called Pingotec. This mosaic art form is made from text and pictures. Each poster is made using a related topic, allowing you to design an exclusive one-of-a-kind personalization for your partner. You can pick the small pictures by one or more specific subjects, like roses, chocolate, wine, or almost anything else. Say it with pictures! (250) 477-1812 – www.pingotec.com
(Mention coupon code MM1 62 and receive a 10% discount.)

188. "Ain't No Mountain High Enough!" While this did take some planning and special permission, it didn't cost any more than a night in a 5 star hotel with room service. Many people may not know this, but you can actually rent beds; the rental company will deliver, set up, and remove the bed. Okay, let me set the scene for you… Imagine being blindfolded with a silk scarf and being whisked away; when the scarf is unveiled, you open your eyes and find yourself at your most favorite place of tranquility, and to the sight of a lone canopy bed gracing the top of a mountain (okay, it was a really big foothill) with a backdrop of the lost and sunken city. A netted style canopy allows for a clear top view to stargaze and dream in each other's arms. Your favorite meal, from your favorite elegant restaurant has been delivered especially for you, to the foothills! (Make arrangements with the restaurant, supplying them with a map and cell phone number, your menu selections, delivery time, and a nice tip. Or, have a friend pick up the order for you and deliver it to your special location.) Your evening is complete - slow dancing beneath a ceiling of stars, sipping wine, eating strawberries, and holding each other close while stargazing. The stars atop a mountain seem close enough to reach out and touch.

189. The sound of love. Arrange for a sweet serenade or madrigal accompanied by lutes, minstrels, a string quartet, tenors, or bagpipes to act as your partner's alarm clock for a day. Hire the musicians to begin playing outside of your sweetheart's bedroom window early one summer morning so your sweetie will awake to these beautiful sounds on his or her special day. If you are musically inclined, gently wake him/her with the lyres or strings from your own musical talent.

190. This is dedicated to the one I love. Dedicate "your song" to your sweetheart on a radio station that he or she will be listening to on the commute to work.

191. La La Means I Love You. Sing a Karaoke song to your leading lady/man. But don't just take the stage and sing "your" song to an audience like so many do, approach your sweetheart, take his/her hand and literally sing "your" song to him/her, perhaps on one knee...

192. Your song. Don't say it, sing it. Hire a songsmith. I have personal experience with this company. The Creative Works will help you put your thoughts to music. Choose one of three unique services:

1. A personal song $75.00. In their Personal Song category, they currently hold 15 songs. These songs can be chosen from the Personalized Song Questionnaire where bits of information are taken from the questionnaire and placed within the song. This order can be taken over the phone. (2-3 weeks for delivery)

2. Original Lyric Song $97.00. In their Original Lyric category, they have an extensive library of original music to which they can fit a completely new and personalized lyric. A variety of styles are available. (2-3 weeks for delivery)

3. Original Music & Lyric Song $175.00. Some of you may desire an Original Music and Lyric Song that is written for him or her in a style modeled on a song of their choice. (3-4 weeks for delivery)

All songs can, of course, be recorded with male or female vocal. Songs are provided on CD accompanied by a lyric sheet. Rush orders are accepted for an additional fee.

Jim Rickert
The Creative Works
617-471-8800
(Mention Romance-411 and receive a 5% discount on any order.)

193. You light up my life. Commemorate a special memory or tender moment with your partner by giving him his own private fireworks display. Bring your lover to that special or secret place he/she loves and celebrate your special occasion or proposed. At a pre-determined time, passionately kiss the lips of your partner and tell him/her that you see fireworks each time that you kiss him/her or let him/her know how he/she lights up your life. Simultaneously, have a Pyro-technician, who is hiding off in the distance, light up the night with your own private firework's show. You will need a permit; most Pyro-technicians will take care of this for you.

While I was hoping to provide you with a single Web address depicting a national registry of Pyro-technicians for a location nearest you, I was unable to find such a list. I was advised by a major firework's company to direct you to your local Fire Department for further guidance regarding permits for pulling off your personalized fireworks show. My local fire department suggested you call:

- The National Licensing Center: 404-417-2750
- The Public Safety Branch: 202-927-2310
- AFT Web site:www.aft.treas.gov

194. Horsing around. If you are planning to celebrate a very special occasion with your sweetheart, rather than renting the traditional limousine, hire a horse-drawn carriage to deliver you to your favorite destination. These types of buggies ornament many major city corners as well as enhance many vacation hot spots. Pre-arrange to be picked up right in front of your hotel and be transported back in time to your designated restaurant. A horse-drawn carriage ride on a starry summer's night along the waterway is equally mesmerizing as taking one on a powdery white winter's eve with giant descending snow flakes. If you can't afford both a fancy dinner and the carriage ride, at around a dollar a minute, have the chariot take you to McDonalds. Stop along the way and pluck a single daisy, set up a table cloth and light a candle. Have the sweetest romantic meal and don't forget to use your "buy one meal, get one free" coupon from the Entertainment Book.

195. Third time is a charm! My (former) fiancé had arrived back in Hawaii from Wisconsin and was greeted at the airport by a chauffeur holding a sign with his name on it. When he got into the limousine, there was a glass of champagne waiting for him, which held a key at the bottom of the glass. He was dropped off in front of a strange building that towered over a canal and golf course. The bellman greeted him with a note card bearing only the words "Penthouse III." He arrived in front of a door wrapped in Christmas paper with a gigantic bow and a sign across the door that read "Merry Christmas." A gift tag hanging from the door knob invited him inside (key #1). Inside the penthouse waited a bow-tied refill glass of champagne with yet another key in the bottom of that glass. He was instructed to follow a trail of my discarded clothing intermixed with rose petals up the stairway, leading him to the door of the rooftop (key #2). A note card was attached to the door reading "Two down, one to go…the third time will be a charm!" When he entered the roof top, I was waiting for him on a rose-petal covered blanket in the warm late afternoon sun, wearing only a floral lei around my neck that was entwined with a gold key charm necklace, exposing an attached gift card that read "Handle with Love, for this is the key to my heart." (Key #3.)

196. My bag. Create a "bath bag" for your home. A "traveler unraveler" works well, hooks over your bathroom door and instantly doubles as a portable take-along bag for that romantic getaway. Stow items such as massage gels, bath oil, bubbles, beads, regular and floating candles, an inflatable bath pillow, food coloring, a baggie filled with dried or satin rose petals, truth or dare cards or dice, little plastic eggs or balls for floating suggestive messages to your partner in the hot tub, a bell, and padded eye cover, etc.

197. Bag of tricks. Always be ready for romance. Keep a romantic "treasure chest" on hand. Use an old suitcase for accessing your "bag of tricks." Stow away secured in the closet or underneath your bed. Suggested items to have on hand, only to name a few: Your official copy of Romance-411™, love coupons, a variety of greeting cards to accommodate all moods and occasions, some small gifts and trinkets, plastic storage eggs, fine fabric or velvet for wrapping special gifts, tissue paper and envelopes, ribbons and bows and all the makings for presenting a beautiful gift. Use separate craft or shoe boxes to store things like your glitter, markers, crayons, designing scissors, glue, glue dots, lighter for burning edges, and candle wax, for sealing love-letters.

198. Guppy love. Write out each of the letters of the alphabet on separate squares of paper and fold them in half. Place them all in an empty fish bowl and decorate (bow, ribbon, special message, your names in a heart etc.). Give it to your partner as a gift. An accompanying card should inform your loved one that he or she gets to randomly pick one square from the bowl each _____(week, month, year, or special occasion) and which ever letter he or she draws will correspond with the "Gift Ideas" listed on page 225, in which he or she will receive one surprise romantic gift, outing, gesture, or interlude based on any of the keywords from that letter category within the next 24 hours.

199. Mind-full. Give your partner a break and do something without being asked. Pick up the dry cleaning, wash the car, empty the dishwasher, go grocery shopping, start or pick up dinner, take out the trash, finish an unfinished project that you promised so long ago etc...

200. My baby just a sent me a letter. Hand pen a good ole fashioned love-letter for your sweetheart.

"In art, the hand can never execute anything higher
Than the heart can inspire."
-Ralph Waldo Emerson

Here is an easy to follow formula for crafting a love-letter. Pick and choose which options will work for you and keep in mind that there is no wrong way to write a love-letter. Writing a love-letter is not about finding or using the right words, but rather, about the love, feeling, emotion, and the intent beneath those words. The heart of the matter is love, and as a first class romantic, I want to be the ambassador in promoting the importance of enriching and stretching your romantic capabilities in your relationship. There is nothing wrong or embarrassing in exposing your emotions and expressing your love to another. It is okay to be vulnerable; there is growth inside of vulnerability - relationship growth and personal growth. If you feel beautiful things and write what you feel, your love-letter will be beautiful. I'm going to spend a little time on love-letters because it is a gift that is often neglected yet means so much to the person receiving it. There is no price you can put on a gift that is spoken from the heart.

1. Find a quiet space to write in, unless you are one of those people who think or write better with your favorite music playing softly in the background.

2. Light a candle and set the mood.

3. Give your full attention, off with the cell phone and TV.

4. Place a picture of the one you love in front of you as inspiration for your letter.

5. Write your rough draft(s) on scratch paper so you can make changes accordingly, saving your fine stationary or parchment for the final draft.

6. Tell him or her how you feel. Begin making an "admiration list." Simply list all of the aspects you most admire, love, and appreciate about your partner. How your partner complements your life or raises the bar for you. List your favorite moments, touches that gave you

goose bumps, memories, times, places, hopes and dreams, firsts for your relationship, etc. Include why he/she means so much to you, has changed your life, etc. Finally, list your hopes and dreams for the future together. Be sure to touch on his/her mental, physical, and spiritual qualities.

7. Begin by personalizing the love-letter with an appropriate salutation for your relationship. Such as:

My Darling __________,

My Heart, My Love,

My Dearest __________,

My Angel,

My Everything,

8. Review your "admiration list" and select your favorites to include in the body of the love-letter. Perhaps begin by telling your love what makes him or her so special to you. Describe how you feel when he/she touches, kisses, caresses, loves, or talks to you and whatever else you feel moved to share.

9. You could conclude your love-letter by sharing your future desires.

10. Personalize the closing of the letter with a heartfelt term of endearment, such as:

I long for your touch,

I can't wait to see you at the altar,

Unconditionally,

Forever,

Forever Yours,

Always or All Ways,

I will love you always,

Your loving Husband,

Your Loving Wife,

I miss every moment I am not with you,

My heart is yours,

It is you and no other,

Until we meet again,

11. Check your letter for errors.

12. Final draft: Use your finest stationery and penmanship and transform your rough draft into a Shakespearean (okay, a cherished) piece of art!

13. Hand-sign your love-letter.

14. You can go as far as soaking your love-letter in hot tea for an early century look and feel; once the paper dries, don't forget to carefully and strategically burn the edges with a lighter.

15. Lightly spray the love-letter with his/her favorite fragrance of yours to remind him/her of you.

16. Insert heart-shaped confetti sprinkles, rose petals, or some other thoughtful sentiment.

17. Gingerly fold your love-letter in half with the text on the inside. Place it in the envelope with the crease at the bottom and the salutation facing the back.

18. Address, seal, and stamp the love-letter:

A.) Seal all of your love-letters with nostalgic sealing wax and secure your own personalized embossed seal onto it. (See the following details.) Or, consider sealing your letter with a coin; perhaps you could use a foreign coin that you picked up together on vacation.

B.) Ladies, seal the envelope with a lipstick kiss!

C.) Pick out a significant stamp for your love-letter at the post office, such as "I Love You" or "Be Mine."

D.) Since the days of war, soldiers would send their sweetheart's letters with the stamp turned upside down as an endearing gesture to say "I love you" and make the letter more personal than just a piece of mailed paper with words on it. Securing your stamp diagonally, says "I miss you."

19. Drop the love-letter in the mail, and look forward to collecting some "passion points."

20. Have your partner sign for the letter to add to the formality of the mail delivery.

Suggestion: If you have undecipherable penmanship, you should probably use a word processor to compose your love-letter and print it off on your finest paper.

One love-letter that I wrote in this fashion was called "101 Things I Love About You." A photo of us was centered on the page and each of the 101 numbered reasons wrapped the space around it. It was delivered in a fanciful frame and was, naturally, wrapped in my signature baby's breath, rose petals, and velvet gift wrap.

Idea: Another neat idea regarding "love-letters" is to send one to your partner's parents. Thank them for bringing your special person into the world and instilling in him or her the qualities that you have grown to love so much.

To view famous love-letters and gather format and style ideas: www.theromantic.com

For a nice collection of writing supplies and embossers:
www.oldschoolseals.com

For an assortment of wax seals and sealing wax:
www.swordmark.com

Wax Seals

Will my wax seal survive a trip through the mail?

Wax seals were made to be broken so the letter could be opened easily. Unfortunately, the postal sorting machines tend to rip off or crush wax seals on the outside of an envelope. There are a couple of things you can try to improve your odds of the seal making it in one piece. First, you can make sure the seal is not on the outside of the envelope where it would be in contact with the machines. Put the seal on a letter inside the envelope, or if it must be on the envelope, put that envelope inside another envelope. Second, you can put the words "Hand Cancel" on the envelope and hand it to a human being at the post office. There is a chance that they can try to bypass the machine.

Wax hardens before I can press the seal into it. What do I do?

This happens for one of two reasons. Either you waited too long after melting the wax before you pressed the seal into it, or you dripped the wax in one spot. If you waited too long, then next time have the seal nearby and ready to use before you melt the wax. After you have blown out the flame, immediately press your seal into the hot wax and wait about 5 seconds before you pull it out.

If you dripped all the wax in one spot hoping to get a big enough puddle to make a seal, the wax will harden long before you get to that point. Sealing wax is very thick and it doesn't flow quickly like candle wax. See the step by step directions below.

Wax is stuck to my seal. How do I get it out?

Do not try to burn the wax out of the seal. That will damage your seal. Let the wax cool and use a pin to poke out the wax or freeze it and it should fall right off. In the olden days, people used to lick the seal or dip it in water before each use. The thin coating of water would keep the hot wax from sticking to the metal. We suggest you lightly spray the metal seal with a non-stick lubricant or cooking spray to ensure that the wax won't stick to the seal. Pay close attention to the areas where the wax stuck and try to lubricate those areas more thoroughly.

Is there any way to reuse the wax from my practice seals?

Yes, you can reuse the wax! Gather all the wax from the ruined seals together and put it into a pan or a spoon (or something that you can apply heat to without ruining). Melt the wax under a flame and gently pour it on your paper where you want your seal. Then press the prepared seal into the wax. Presto! You have successfully recycled the wax from earlier attempts. If you are using wax seal ink (to make a two-tone seal), do not spray the seal. The pigment in the ink will act as the lubricant.

"A little seal, so romantic and chaste.
A symbol of beauty, elegance, and taste."

To cleanup, wipe the metal seal with a paper towel. If any wax is stuck to the metal, use a pin to poke it out, and next time lubricate that spot more carefully.

These great tips on wax seals were compiled for the education and convenience of those who want to reference them, brought to you by: www.swordmark.com

	Step 1	Light the wax, tilt the stick at an angle, and let the wax drip where you want your seal.
	Step 2	Start by creating a circle of wax slightly larger than your seal.
	Step 3	Next, fill in the circle and blow out the wax stick. You can use the back end of your wax stick to stir the wax if it has not dripped uniformly.
	Step 4	Place the metal seal firmly in the wax while it is still liquid. Wait 5 seconds to allow the wax to harden before pulling the seal from the wax.

Your A – Z Guide To Gift Giving

"Gifts are bookmarks that tell those we love where they appeared in the story written upon our hearts."

–Sgt. Traci

Your A – Z Guide to Gift Giving

A	Attention, Albums, Aphrodisiacs, Art Gallery, Azaleas, Artwork, Antiques, Accolades, A` La Mode, Athens, Australia
B	Backrubs, Balloons, Breakfast In Bed, Baked Goods, Bubble Bath (Together), Bike Ride, Body Shots, Board Games, Books, Boat Ride, Ballet Tickets, Ball Park Tickets, Beach Trip, Bed & Breakfast, Barry White, Broadway
C	Cuddle Time, Crabtree & Evelyn, Conversation, Cookies, Cook Together, Cards, Candles, Cds, Chocolates, Concert Tickets, Couples Yoga/massage Class, Canoeing, Community Project, Carriage Ride, Camping, Carnival, Champagne, Caviar, Cigars, Cuff Links, Collectables, Cruise, Car, Casablanca, Chilvary
D	Date Night, Dance Together (In The Kitchen-with No Music), Doughnuts, Day In Bed, Dedicate A Song, Dance Classes, Dining Out, Diamonds , Daffodils, Daisies
E	Evening Strolls, Endearing Messages, Earrings, Erotica, Escape Weekends, Engagement Rings, Emeralds
F	Free Time, French Kisses, Five Star Treatment, Fortune Cookie, Films, Flowers, Fruits, Fan Merchandise, Fragrance, Flask (Engraved), Family Portrait, Furs, Furniture, Fulfill a Fantacy, France
G	Giggling, Gift Certificates, Go Apple or Strawberry Picking, Garter Belts, Gourmet Recipes and Gadgets, Glassware, Golfing or Golf Goods, Guitars, Gemstones, Gold, Gondola Ride, Godiva, Glen Miller, Greece, Go-Karting
H	Holding Hands, Hand Massages, Hugs, Hot Chocolate by The Fire, Hersey's Kisses, Hawaii, Heart to Heart Talks, Hiking, Husband of The Year Award, Hats, Hayride, Heart-Shaped Things, Health Club Membership, Hot Air Balloon Ride, Horseback Riding, Hotel Stays, Honeymoons (2nd, 3rd, Etc.)
I	Invitation, Intimacy, Ice Cream, Incense, Ice Skating, Island Vacations, Italy

J	Jokes, Jazz Music, Jewelry Box, Jewelry, Java, Jasmine, Jacuzzi
K	Kiss, Kindness, King For A Day, Kite, Kitten, Kitchen Remodel
L	Laughter, Listen to Music, Licorice, Lingerie, Love Poetry, Letters and Songs, Lap Dance, Lobster Gram, Leather Goods, Limousines, London, Lace, Lilacs
M	Massages, Manicures, Make Love, Magic Beans, Message In A Bottle, Movie Rental, Movie Tickets, Mugs, Miniature Golf, Museums, Magazine Subscriptions, Music, Moonlight, Musicals, Money Clip (Engraved), Marriage Proposal, Mountains , Mozart
N	Nurture, Night Time Stroll or Swim, Night of Cuddling or Passion, Nightgowns, Novels, Necklaces, Name A Star After Your Sweetie, New Outfit, Nature Escapes, National Park, Napa Valley, Nepal, Nightcap, Negligee
O	Office Call ("I'm Thinking Of You"), Ornaments, Opera Tickets, Opals, Oil Painting, Orchid, Outdoors, Outfit, Outting
P	Party (Surprise), Pick Wild Flowers, Pedicures, Picnics in the Park, Popcorn, Pajamas, Perfume, Picnic Baskets, Poetry, Plays, Personalized Gifts, Pottery, Photos, Pizza, Paris, Pearls, Polka, Panties
Q	Quality Time, Quiet Afternoons, Quit A Bad Habit, Queen For A Day, Quilts (Handmade or Personalized)
R	Read Together, Rest & Relaxation Day, Roller Skating, Root Beer Float & Two Straws, Roses, Robes, Rings, Row Boat, Rugs, Rome, Rio, Riviera, Rubies
S	Set A Goal Together, Spa Treatments At Home, Skinny Dip, Star Gaze, Strip Poker, Self Portrait, Surprise Party, Satin Sheets, Strawberries & Champagne, Stuffed Animals, Scrapbook, Stamps, Silk, Symphony Tickets, Summer Outfit, Spa Visit, Sailing Trips, Shopping Spree, Sight Seeing, Sade (CD)

T	Tucked in Bed, Time Together, T-Shirts, Tattoos, Theater Trip, Teapots and Gourmet Teas, Telegram, Teddy Bear, Tie, Tie Clip (Engraved), Tools, Tickets, Tents, Travel Together
U	Unconditional Love, Umbrellas
V	Visit With Each Other, Visit A Favorite Place, Votive Candles, Vases, Vineyards, Vintage Gifts, Vacations, Violets, Venice, Victoria's Secret
W	Watch Sunsets and Sunrises, Workout Together, Watch A Movie, Wife Of The Year Award, Watches (Engraved), Wine Tasting, Waterfall Trips, Weekend Getaways, When Harry Met Sally Movie
X	Extravagant Gifts & Gestures, Extra Time & Attention
Y	"Your Day-your Way" Coupon, Yarn & Craft Supplies, "YES" (Let your sweetie have their way today), Yoga Class, Yachts
Z	Zen Time, Zoo Trips, Zippo Lighter (Engraved), Zanzibar

Tips: Know your partner's sizes: ring finger, neck, shirt, pant, dress, hat, coat, shoe, and under garment. Keep a list in your wallet so you can buy a gift that fits anytime you're out!

Be creative and surprise your partner with gifts for no reason at all! A gift that is given sincerely does not have to be expensive to speak volumes to the recipient.

Sgt. Traci's Web Picks for Romantic Gifts:

My favorite website for gift shopping! FindGift.com is a free service that helps you find unique gift ideas and connects you to online stores where these gifts are sold. They search the web to bring you great gift ideas!
www.findgift.com

The Place for Bridal, Wedding, and Romantic Gifts.
www.onepassionplace.com

Looking for wedding ideas, advice, or expertise about the wedding ceremony, cake, flowers, gifts, music, photos, videos, wedding party members' responsibilities, and more? This site has unique wedding ideas will help you plan for the wedding of your dreams.
www.allweddingideas.com

The following site offers a nice assortment of lingerie and standard to exotic romantic gifts.
www.fantasies-in-lace-lingerie.com

Romantic gifts from the heart to suit a variety of occasions can be found on these sites.
www.uncommongoods.com
www.forromance.com
www.links2love.com (Click "Site Index" on the left side of the page.)

An exquisite display of chocolate covered strawberries and wine bottle arrangements.
www.romancestruck.com/shop/chocolate-strawberries.htm

Have a favorite perfume or cologne delivered anytime.
www.perfumemania.com
Nice therapeutic gifts that can be used at home or at the office.
www.brookstone.com

For an assortment of body pampering items and gift baskets try these sites.
www.crabtree-evelyn.com
www.bodyshop.com

Neat personalized gifts can be found at:
www.syxy.com/guideweb/ (Click on shopping/gifts.)

Order your love flowers and have them delivered anywhere at any time!
1-800-736-3383 — www.FTG.com
www.1800flowers.com

For the finest in Chocolates, delivered fresh to your door:
www.godiva.com

This site features the highest quality hand rolled cigars. You can also customize your cigars with a label of your choice or have your own label designed.
www.littlecigarfactory.com

This site offers unique, trend-setting ideas for party favors and gifts, sure to give you new ideas for the wedding, shower, or special party you are planning.
www.beau-coup.com

For a larger collection of romantic ideas with a larger variety of less expensive alternatives here are a few of my personal favorite romantic resources, each offering a collection of neat gift ideas, recipes, and stories that enlighten and inspire.
www.links2love.com
www.romancestuck.com
www.theromantic.com

1001 Ways to be Romantic by Greg Godek, is another book resource that is packed with 1001 ways to be romantic with ideas designed to accommodate everyone's budget.

Gift Wrapping Ideas

"The gifts we bear to those we love are woven into the lives of those who love us."

–Sgt. Traci

Of course, when you give a gift you have to wrap it! And in my opinion, presentation is everything! If you are going to put effort, time, love, and expense into a romantic gift, then go all the way and put some effort in the gift presentation itself. Give a gift that looks so beautiful that your partner will not even want to open it!

Here are some of my signature gift wrapping suggestions:

Line the bottom of a gift box in velvet or crushed penne fabric (this is a less expensive alternative to velvet and in my opinion, is equally beautiful and elegant) available at your local fabric store. Place the box on top of the reverse side of the fabric, using a fabric marker trace the outline of the box, cut the fabric, check to make sure the fabric fits neatly in the bottom of the box, then secure it with fabric glue or gummy-glue dots. (Gummy dots work very well to secure fabric to a box or fabric to fabric, although double-sided tape also works, it is a bit tedious to work with.)

Sprinkle rose petals or miniature roses inside. I like to re-gift my roses by giving the same ones back that were once given to me by the gift recipient. I tack each of them down, one by one to the fabric and tissue paper, using a gummy glue dot.

Wrap the gift in fine tissue, velvet, or crushed pen ne fabric and secure the wrapping with a fancy rope tie or ribbon.

Spray it with a faint whisper of his/her favorite cologne or perfume.

Add more rose petals atop and secure with gummy glue dots.

Trimming your gift with a hand-tied ribbon creates a beautiful effect. If you do not know how to do this, bring your gift to your local florist, and for a fee, you will receive an award-winning ribbon presentation. Chain craft stores such as "Hobby Lobby" and "Michael's" occasionally offer one session ribbon tying classes. (In fact, I will be teaching one in my area.)

Use wax to seal all of your cards and gift-cards.

Write out your cards and envelopes using calligraphy.

Inlaid wisps of greenery will enhance any gift. Or, you can place your tissue-wrapped gift on a bed of potpourri, wheat strands, wild flowers, cat-tails, baby's breath, fern fronds, autumn leaves, or pussy willows.

Use velvet or your left-over penne fabric for wrapping "gift" bottles. Simply place your bottle on a piece of 25" x 25" (accommodates most bottle sizes) square of fabric and lift the four corners to meet at the top of the bottle. Secure the fabric at the neck of the bottle with a twist-tie, thin ribbon, or a rubber band and then add a beautiful hand-tied bow or ribbon over it, and add a gift tag.

Add any personal or sentimental trimmings and tie it into your hand-tied ribbon and bow, for example tassels for graduation, mini nautical rope for the yachtsman, baby booties for the mother- to-be, or mistletoe and pine cones during the holidays.

If you can spare the expense and like to stand out from the rest, "think outside the box" and have all your gift/shirt/sweater boxes embossed with your initials or your family coat of arms.

“Us” Begins With “U”

SGT. TRACI HAS CRACKED THE ROMANCE CODE!

"The secret to having a happy and healthy relationship is to have a happy and healthy you!" -Sgt. Traci

SECRET FORMULA FOR HAPPY COUPLE-HOOD

$((Y + SL) \times (SW + SE) \times (F^3) + (Y + M) \times (F) \times (T + I) \times (T + A) \times (B + C) \times (C^3 + C^3) \times (M + A)\sqrt{(H \times T + A + P)} = \text{TRUE ROMANCE}))$

Decoded:

(You + Self Love) x (Self Worth + Self Esteem) x (Forgiveness of Self + Others) + (You + Me) x (Friendship) x (Thought + Imagination) x (Time^2 + Attention) x (Budget + Creativity^3) x (Communication + Commitment) x (Mood + Atmosphere) x (Honesty^2 + Trust) x (Affection + Pampering.) = True Romance

Give your partner the greatest and most romantic gift of all...a new and improved you! Make some changes. Relationship experts claim that when you make motions to improve and change your own life, your surrounding relationships will also improve and change. Be the one to raise the bar for your loved ones. Don't allow anyone to be less than who you know he or she is or be and do less than what you know he or she is capable of achieving, especially yourself. It is easy to get caught up and then eventually stuck in routines, comfort zones, and sitting on idle in your life, job, and relationship.

"Doing something small is better than doing nothing at all!" My own personal quote and words that I live by. Shave off your mustache or at least groom it, sport a new look or style, reach over and deliver a soul-stirring French kiss to your lover while you are going through the automatic car wash, take a new route to work, run around the block, wake up and dance a jig in the kitchen while you are making your coffee, sign up for a class, learn a new craft, set a goal, create an action plan, or do yourself the ultimate favor and forgive an ill will or an old debt..... It doesn't matter what it is, just do something different today. If you want something different, you have to do something different. Don't think about it, just go do it! As Einstein once said, "Nothing happens without movement." Move! When you do something different, you will begin to feel different and your peers will begin to see you differently. When you feel better, the people around you will treat you better. Your relationship with your partner and your peers will be better. I believe that when one makes a commitment to the simple act of following through on anything that they start, things will begin to happen for them.

Start simple. Don't overload yourself. Set a goal and take at least one action towards achieving that goal each day (See goal setting template beginning on page 301).

The Economics of "U"

The amount of self-love, self-worth, and self-esteem a person has is in direct proportion to how much it costs anyone to be in a relationship with him or her. The amount of self-love is subject to the same pressures of supply and demand as any other commodity and thus can be measured with a simple economics chart. As your supply of self-love, self-worth, and self-esteem in a relationship increases, that line moves to the right on the chart, and the cost or the price that someone would have to pay emotionally and physically to be involved with you decreases. The result is that the quality of the relationship, the line along the bottom of the chart shows an increase. The converse is also true. If the supply of self-love, self-worth, and self-esteem in your relationship decreases, the chart reveals that the line moves to the left, and the price to be involved with you increases and the quality of the relationship decreases.

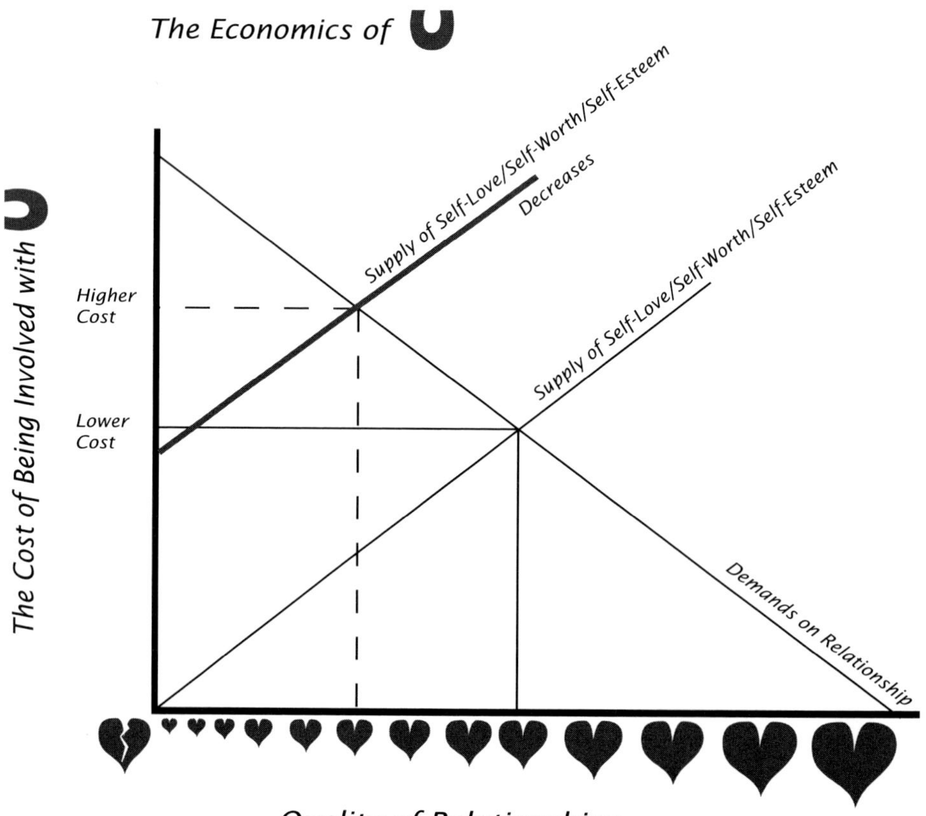

"US" Begins With "U".

Mirror Mirror On The Wall... When I returned home after traveling the world and discovering truths about human relationships and about myself, I knew I wanted to share what I had learned in order to open up others' perceptions of what romance could be.

This book was conceived, half on the pain of heartbreak and half on an attempt to win back the love I had lost. It practically wrote itself as I poured myself into it for fourteen to sixteen hours a day until I thought I had nothing left to give and nothing left to grieve, but still I did not publish it and I didn't know why; I was still empty and hurting. The "finished" but unsettled manuscript sat, touched only by particles of dust, for more than a year. One day, I picked it up and re-read it from cover to cover and had one of the greatest epiphanies of my life! That manuscript (this book) had inadvertently become the mirror into my soul, and as I read it with misty eyes, I understood that the element that had been missing the whole while in completing this book and closing my own personal chapter on lost romance, was ME! It awakened me to face the mirror and see that the true secret to having a happy and healthy relationship is to first have a happy and healthy self and that all these sweet and thoughtful "Hollywood style" romantic gestures were just the icing on the cake, not the foundation on which a relationship can sustain itself. I realized why I had been unable to experience the true romance I had dreamed about on those cold nights in far away lands and struggled to create externally here at home. I knew at that moment the only way I was going to be able to experience, teach, and be in love was to start right here in this book, inside of myself. That "Us Begins With U"; begins with me, begins with you. Yes, all the things I have written about here can and will accentuate that loving relationship, even breathe new life into an old one so long as you have a solid foundation to spread the icing upon.

While navigating the world, I learned the importance of knowing where I was and where I needed to go. This is also true as we navigate through our various relationships in life. While there are many styles or kinds of relationships in our lives, among the most sacred is the relationship we have with our source, ourselves, and with our life partner. In order to continually build, improve, or strengthen these relationships, a great idea to consider would be implementing an annual relationship report or yearly report card if you will, of your significant relationship and of your significant self. After all, we spend all year planning for the end of the year with annual reports and expense accounts to be turned in for evaluation at year's end, we set personal New Year resolutions and business goals, we bring in our automobiles for tune-ups, give "peer reviews," and schedule our annual check-ups of our bodies and teeth. But how often do we review our relationship or goals within it or give our relationships a check-up, let alone a tune-up?

This next section is not meant to point out one's flaws or short comings or make you or your partner feel bad. It is strictly intended to be used as a navigational compass of where you are from where you want to be or would like to be in your relationship. There is nothing wrong or derogatory about having an annual "relationship report" discussion to gage where you are or where you want to be next year at the same time, set goals (both as a couple and personally), or simply just to ensure that you are both on the same page.

Give it a try! Rate yourself and ask your partner to rate you or rate each other on a scale of 1-5 with 1 being low, 3 being average and 5 being high. Access where you think you or each other are at and circle which rating number applies. Compare the differences or similarities in your answers and set some relationship and/or perhaps some personal goals to strive for based on the outcome.

Like I mentioned earlier, the greatest gift to everyone in your life, is a new and improved you! This "relationship report" is something to think about and you just might learn something about yourself or your significant relationship that you never really thought about or realized before. Be truthful; be vulnerable when you ask yourself these questions. The questions aren't tough, but the answers might be! Only you know your own truth and only you are capable of changing it.

Mirror-Mirror On The Wall...	(List name of self or person grading or being graded here)	(List name of self or person grading or being graded here)
1. Ability to Give Love	1 2 3 4 5	1 2 3 4 5
2. Ability to Receive Love	1 2 3 4 5	1 2 3 4 5
3. Ability to Be Loving	1 2 3 4 5	1 2 3 4 5
4. The Friend in You	1 2 3 4 5	1 2 3 4 5
5. The Lover in You	1 2 3 4 5	1 2 3 4 5
6. Love Making Skills	1 2 3 4 5	1 2 3 4 5
7. Sexual Satisfaction To Partner	1 2 3 4 5	1 2 3 4 5
8. Non-Sexual Intimacy	1 2 3 4 5	1 2 3 4 5
9. Affectionate	1 2 3 4 5	1 2 3 4 5
10. Listening Skills	1 2 3 4 5	1 2 3 4 5
11. Communication Skills	1 2 3 4 5	1 2 3 4 5
12. Ability to Express Your Feelings	1 2 3 4 5	1 2 3 4 5
13. Keeping Your Word /Accountability	1 2 3 4 5	1 2 3 4 5
14. Commitment Ability	1 2 3 4 5	1 2 3 4 5

15. Are You Always Right & Never Wrong	1 2 3 4 5	1 2 3 4 5
16. Need to Prove Others Wrong or Self Right	1 2 3 4 5	1 2 3 4 5
17. Problem Solving	1 2 3 4 5	1 2 3 4 5
18. Argumentative	1 2 3 4 5	1 2 3 4 5
19. Demanding/Dominant	1 2 3 4 5	1 2 3 4 5
20. Forgiving/Resolution	1 2 3 4 5	1 2 3 4 5
21. Stubborn/ Close Minded	1 2 3 4 5	1 2 3 4 5
22. Easy Going/ Open Minded	1 2 3 4 5	1 2 3 4 5
23. Criticize vs. Compliment	1 2 3 4 5	1 2 3 4 5
24. Compliment vs. Criticize	1 2 3 4 5	1 2 3 4 5
25. Integrity	1 2 3 4 5	1 2 3 4 5
26. Trusting	1 2 3 4 5	1 2 3 4 5
27. Distrusting	1 2 3 4 5	1 2 3 4 5
28. Patience	1 2 3 4 5	1 2 3 4 5
29. Angry/violent	1 2 3 4 5	1 2 3 4 5

30. Jealous	1 2 3 4 5	1 2 3 4 5
31. Insecure	1 2 3 4 5	1 2 3 4 5
32. Content	1 2 3 4 5	1 2 3 4 5
33. Happy	1 2 3 4 5	1 2 3 4 5
34. Distant	1 2 3 4 5	1 2 3 4 5
35. Selfish	1 2 3 4 5	1 2 3 4 5
36. Involved	1 2 3 4 5	1 2 3 4 5
37. Ambitious	1 2 3 4 5	1 2 3 4 5
38. Lazy	1 2 3 4 5	1 2 3 4 5
39. Hygienic of Self & Home	1 2 3 4 5	1 2 3 4 5
40. Flexibility	1 2 3 4 5	1 2 3 4 5
41. Stability	1 2 3 4 5	1 2 3 4 5
42. Considerate	1 2 3 4 5	1 2 3 4 5
43. Caring	1 2 3 4 5	1 2 3 4 5
44. Fairness	1 2 3 4 5	1 2 3 4 5

45. Punctuality	1 2 3 4 5	1 2 3 4 5
46. Thoughtfulness	1 2 3 4 5	1 2 3 4 5
47. Generous	1 2 3 4 5	1 2 3 4 5
48. Greedy	1 2 3 4 5	1 2 3 4 5
49. Receiving	1 2 3 4 5	1 2 3 4 5
50. Giving	1 2 3 4 5	1 2 3 4 5
51. Romantic in Words, Deeds, Gestures, & Gifts	1 2 3 4 5	1 2 3 4 5
52. Playful	1 2 3 4 5	1 2 3 4 5
53. Adventuresome or Spontaneity	1 2 3 4 5	1 2 3 4 5
54. Couch Potato or Complacency	1 2 3 4 5	1 2 3 4 5
55. Take On New Challenges	1 2 3 4 5	1 2 3 4 5
56. Live In Comfort Zone, Auto Pilot, or "Ground Hog Day"	1 2 3 4 5	1 2 3 4 5
57. Takes Risks	1 2 3 4 5	1 2 3 4 5
58. Open To or Seeks New Challenges	1 2 3 4 5	1 2 3 4 5
59. Sense of Humor	1 2 3 4 5	1 2 3 4 5

60. Sensitivity	1 2 3 4 5	1 2 3 4 5
61. Tolerance	1 2 3 4 5	1 2 3 4 5
62. Judgment	1 2 3 4 5	1 2 3 4 5
63. Gossiper/ Spread Ill Will	1 2 3 4 5	1 2 3 4 5
64. Talk the Talk (full of excuses and blame)	1 2 3 4 5	1 2 3 4 5
65. Walk the Walk (full of action & results)	1 2 3 4 5	1 2 3 4 5
66. Loyalty	1 2 3 4 5	1 2 3 4 5
67. Personal Growth	1 2 3 4 5	1 2 3 4 5
68. Personal Fulfillment	1 2 3 4 5	1 2 3 4 5
69. Relationship Fulfillment	1 2 3 4 5	1 2 3 4 5
70. Career Fulfillment	1 2 3 4 5	1 2 3 4 5
71. Spiritual Health	1 2 3 4 5	1 2 3 4 5
72. Physical Health	1 2 3 4 5	1 2 3 4 5
73. Emotional Health	1 2 3 4 5	1 2 3 4 5
74. Mental Health	1 2 3 4 5	1 2 3 4 5

75. Financial Health and Retirement	1 2 3 4 5	1 2 3 4 5
76. Financially Responsible	1 2 3 4 5	1 2 3 4 5
77. Would your partner say that you make him/her feel sexy?	1 2 3 4 5	1 2 3 4 5
78. Would your partner say that he/she feels appreciated by you?	1 2 3 4 5	1 2 3 4 5
79. Would your partner say that he/she feels wanted by you?	1 2 3 4 5	1 2 3 4 5
80. Would your partner say that he/she feels needed by you?	1 2 3 4 5	1 2 3 4 5
81. Would your partner say that he/she feels loved by you?	1 2 3 4 5	1 2 3 4 5
82. Would your partner say that he/she feels desired by you?	Yes or No	Yes or No
83. Would your partner say that he/she feels cherished by you?	Yes or No	Yes or No
84. Would your partner say that he/she feels admired by you?	Yes or No	Yes or No
85. Would your partner say that he/she feels respected by you?	Yes or No	Yes or No
86. Would your partner say that he/she feels happy that he/she committed to or married you?	Yes or No	Yes or No
87. Would your partner say that he/she often feels invisible?	Yes or No	Yes or No

88. Would your partner say that he/she feels support from you?	Yes or No	Yes or No
89. Would your partner say that he/she feels important to you?	Yes or No	Yes or No
90. Would your partner say that he/she feels valuable to you?	Yes or No	Yes or No
91. Would your partner say that he/she feels attractive to you?	Yes or No	Yes or No
92. Would your partner say that he/she feels listened to/heard by you?	Yes or No	Yes or No
93. Would your partner say that he/she still feels like you are still friends?	Yes or No	Yes or No
94. Are you missing the bulls-eye in your relationship?	Yes or No	Yes or No
95.What do you bring to your relationship?		
96. Are you a dream builder or are you a dream destroyer when it comes to your partner? Yourself? Others?		
97. What do you want? What do you really want?		
98. What fear stops you from following through on what you say that you want?		
99. If failure was not an option, where would you be right now?		

100. What pleasure do you get from not following through on what you say that you want? (And there is at least one!)		
101. What are you missing out on by not taking the actions necessary in getting what you say that you want?		

Nobody is perfect and we all have room for improvement in some area of our life. Only you know your own truth and know whether or not you are satisfied or disappointed with your rating. Are you living your life by that of choice and design or by way of reaction and circumstances? Remember, if you want major change in your life and in your relationships, you have to make major changes in yourself and in your lifestyle! It is never about anyone else, the mirror always reflects back on you! Everything that happens in your life begins with you and is your responsibility. I am not saying that you are responsible for another person's inflictions, but certainly you are responsible for how you choose to handle them, how well you tolerate them, and for how long! Only you know what you need to do from here!

"What was does not have to be what is" -Sgt. Traci

Official Romance-411 Reference Directory

Table of Contents

Anniversary Coordinates

"No man has ever looked back on his life and said "I loved too much."

–Sgt. Traci

Anniversary Coordinates:

Anniversary	Traditional	Modern
First	Paper	Clocks
Second	Cotton	China
Third	Leather	Crystal/Glass
Fourth	Fruit	Appliances
Fifth	Wood	Silverware
Sixth	Candy	Wood
Seventh	Wool	Desk Sets
Eighth	Bronze	Linens/Lace
Ninth	Pottery	Leather
Tenth	Tin/Aluminum	Diamond Jewelry
Eleventh	Steel	Fashion Jewelry
Twelfth	Silk/Linen	Pearls
Thirteenth	Lace	Textiles/Furs
Fourteenth	Ivory	Gold Jewelry
Fifteenth	Crystal	Watches
Twentieth	China	Platinum
Twenty-Fifth	Silver	Silver
Thirtieth	Pearl	Diamond
Thirty-Fifth	Coral	Jade
Fortieth	Ruby	Ruby
Forty-Fifth	Sapphire	Sappire
Fiftieth	Gold	Gold

Birth Stones

“True strength in any relationship is born of embracing its weaknesses.”

–Sgt. Traci

Birth Stones:

Special thanks to our friends for the following contribution:
www.popculturemadness.com
www.romancestuck.com

The concept of Traditional Birthstones that is commonly referred to today is believed to have originated in the 1500s. Each stone labelled as a birthstone had a symbolic meaning associated with it, which for the superstitious was supposed to bring good fortune to the recipient of the stones. Some believe that the original associations between gemstones and the months of the year evolved from 12 stones mentioned in the Bible. Others say it represents the Twelve Apostles. And still others think that birthstones originated in Jerusalem, where castle walls were decorated with 12 gems, subsequently dividing them into the 12 months. The idea of birthstones is understood the world over although the exact correlation of one birthstone with a particular month varies widely from country to country. In the 18th century, 12 major categories were created, including the Arabian, Hindu, Jewish, Roman, Polish, and Russian categories. In the 20th century, the original local birthstones were further divided into an American and European system.

This Modern Birthstone list is the official birthstone list from the American National Association of Jewelers. It was adopted in the United States in 1912.

Month	Birthstone	Meaning
January	Garnet	Faith & Constancy
February	Amethyst	Happiness & Sincerity
March	Aquamarine	Courage & Hope
April	Diamond	Innocence & Joy
May	Emerald	Peace & Tranquility
June	Pearl	Purity & Wisdom
July	Ruby	Nobility & Passion
August	Peridot	Joy & Power
September	Sapphire	Truth & Hope
October	Opal	Tender Love & Confidence
November	Topaz	Fidelity & Friendship
December	Turquoise	Success & Understanding

Symbolism of Gemstones

“Love is the gemstone we wear around our hearts.”

–Sgt. Traci

Symbolism of Gemstones

Special thanks to our friends for the following contribution:
www.romancestuck.com

Agate: Endows the wearer with calmness, courage, eloquence, health, longevity, virtue, and wealth.Amethyst: Symbolizes deep love, happiness, humility, sincerity, and wealth.

Aquamarine: Believed to ensure continual happiness and constancy in love; symbolizes health, hope, and youth.

Beryl: Symbolizes everlasting youth, happiness, and hope.

Bloodstone: Believed to endow courage, wisdom, and vitality; symbolizes audaciousness, brilliance, courage, generosity, and health.

Carbunkle: Symbolizes constancy, energy, self-confidence, and strength.

Carmelian: Symbolizes courage, joy, friendship, and peace; believed to disperse evil thoughts and sorrow.

Cat's Eye: Symbolizes courage, joy, friendship, and peace; believed to warn its owner of approaching danger.

Chrysoberyl: Symbolizes patience in sorrow.

Chrysolite: Symbolizes disappointed love and wisdom.

Coral: Symbolizes attachment; believed to be an amulet against natural disasters, disease, bad luck, and jealous friends.

Crystal: Symbolizes purity and simplicity.

Diamond: Symbolizes brilliance, constancy, excellence, innocence, invulnerable faith, joy, life, love, and purity.

Emerald: Symbolizes spring, rebirth, hope, peace, and tranquility; believed to endow its wearer with an accommodating and pleasing disposition.

Garnet: Symbolizes constancy, faith, loyalty, and strength; believed to endow its wearer with cheerfulness and sincerity.

Jade: Symbolizes harmonious living, intelligence, longevity, strength, and purity; believed to endow its wearer with good luck and good health; embodies charity, wisdom, courage, justice, and modesty.

Lapis Lazuli: Symbolizes ability, cheerfulness, nobility, and trust, believed to bring its wearer happiness, love, and prosperity.

Moonstone: Symbolizes pensiveness and intelligence; believed to bring its wearer good luck.

Onyx: Symbolizes clearness and dignity; believed to bring its wearer marital bliss.

Opal: Symbolic of confidence, happiness, hope, innocence, prayer, and tender love; believed to endow its wearer with pure thoughts and increased faithfulness.

Pearl: Symbolizes beauty, faithfulness, humility, innocence, integrity, modesty, purity, refinement, wisdom, and wealth.

Peridot: Symbolizes happiness; believed to discourage betrayal and to encourage friendship and marriage.

Ruby: Symbolizes beauty, charity, daintiness, dignity, happiness, love, and passion; believed to have the ability to dispel discord and sadness, to preserve its wearer from false friendships, and to warn of imminent danger.

Sapphire: Symbolizes calmness, constancy, contemplation, hope, innocence, purity, truth, and virtue; believed to bring its wearer comfort, courage, and strength, while pacifying anger, protecting from danger, and fostering constancy in love.

Sardonyx: Symbolizes diving love, marital happiness, vivacity, and power; believed to endow those born under its influence with honesty and mercy.

Topaz: Symbolizes divine goodness, eager love, fidelity, friendship, gentleness, and integrity; believed to bring its wearer recognition, wealth, and protection from evil.

Tourmaline: Symbolizes courage, generosity, and thoughtfulness; believed to bring its wearer happiness and prosperity

Turquoise: Symbolizes earth, happiness, good health, hope, prosperity, and success; considered to be a pledge of friendship when given as a gift.

Zircon: Symbolizes respect; believed to be a charm against jealousy and theft.

Flowers

“Romance is the heat in the air between two lovers.. the moment before their lips meet.”

–Sgt. Traci

Birth Month Flowers:

Special thanks to our friends for the following contribution:
www.romancestuck.com

Birth Month	Flower
January	Carnation
February	Violet
March	Jonquil
April	Sweet Pea
May	Lily of the Valley
June	Rose
July	Larkspur
August	Gladiolus
September	Aster
October	Calendula
November	Chrysanthemum
December	Narcissus

Flower Color Significance:

Special thanks to our friends for the following contribution:
www.romancestuck.com

Flower Color	Meaning
Black	Power, Mystery, Elegance, Farewell
Coral/Peach	Desire, Innocent Love, Wisdom, Gratitude, Appreciation
Blue	Stability, Trustworthy, Tranquil
Dark Pink	Thankfulness
Green	Harmony, Fertility
Lavender/ Purple	Enchanting, Unique, Noble, Devotion
Light Pink	Grace, Gladness, Joy
Orange	Fascination, Warmth, Happiness
Pink	Romance, Sweetness, Playfulness, Gladness
Peach	Appreciation, Admiration or Sympathy
Red	Love, Passion, Desire, Eroticism
White	Purity, Innocence, Perfection, Hope
White & Red	Unity, Togetherness, Long-Lasting Love
Yellow	Friendship, Joy, Happiness

“I Love You” in a Hundred Languages

"Her reflection alone holds the power to leave him dizzy with love, her presence, a fever of passion."

–Sgt. Traci

How to say "I Love you" in 100 Languages

Special thanks to our source for the following contribution:
www.links2love.com

Country	Translation
English	I love you
Afrikaans	Ek het jou lief
Albanian	Te dua
Arabic	Ana behibak (to male)
Arabic	Ana behibek (to female)
Armenian	Yes kez sirumen
Bambara	M'bi fe
Bangla	Aamee tuma ke bhalo aashi
Belarusian	Ya tabe kahayu
Bisaya	Nahigugma ako kanimo
Bulgarian	Obicham te
Cambodian	Soro lahn nhee ah
Cantonese Chinese	Ngo oiy ney a
Catalan	T'estimo
Cheyenne	Ne mohotatse
Chichewa	Ndimakukonda
Corsican	Ti tengu caru (to male)

Country	Translation
Creol	Mi aime jou
Croatian	Volim te
Czech	Miluji te
Danish	Jeg Elsker Dig
Dutch	Ik hou van jou
Elvish	Amin mela lle
Esperanto	Mi amas vin
Estonian	Ma armastan sind
Ethiopian	Afgreki'
Faroese	Eg elski teg
Farsi	Doset daram
Filipino	Mahal kita
Finnish	Mina rakastan sinua
French	Je t'aime, Je t'adore
Frisian	Ik hâld fan dy
Gaelic	Ta gra agam ort
Georgian	Mikvarhar
German	Ich liebe dich
Greek	S'agapo

Country	Translation
Gujarati	Hoo thunay prem karoo choo
Hiligaynon	Palangga ko ikaw
Hawaiian	Aloha Au Ia`oe
Hebrew	Ani ohev otah (to female)
Hebrew	Ani ohev et otha (to male)
Hiligaynon	Guina higugma ko ikaw
Hindi	Hum Tumhe Pyar Karte hae
Hmong	Kuv hlub koj
Hopi	Nu' umi unangwa'ta
Hungarian	Szeretlek
Icelandic	Eg elska tig
Ilonggo	Palangga ko ikaw
Indonesian	Saya cinta padamu
Inuit	Negligevapse
Irish	Taim i' ngra leat
Italian	Ti amo
Japanese	Aishiteru
Kannada	Naanu ninna preetisuttene
Kapampangan	Kaluguran daka

Kiswahili	Nakupenda
Konkani	Tu magel moga cho
Korean	Sarang Heyo
Latin	Te amo
Latvian	Es tevi miilu
Lebanese	Bahibak
Lithuanian	Tave myliu
Luxembourgeois	Ech hun dech gäer
Malay	Saya cintakan mu / Aku cinta padamu
Malayalam	Njan Ninne Premikunnu
Mandarin Chinese	Wo ai ni
Marathi	Me tula prem karto
Mohawk	Kanbhik
Moroccan	Ana moajaba bik
Nahuatl	Ni mits neki
Navaho	Ayor anosh'ni
Norwegian	Jeg Elsker Deg
Pandacan	Syota na kita!!
Pangasinan	Inaru Taka
Papiamento	Mi ta stimabo

Persian	Doo set daaram
Pig Latin	Iay ovlay ouyay
Polish	Kocham Ciebie
Portuguese	Eu te amo
Romanian	Te iubesc
Russian	Ya tebya liubliu
Scot Gaelic	Tha gra\dh agam ort
Serbian	Volim te
Setswana	Ke a go rata
Sign Language	,\,,/ (signing I Love You finger position)
Sindhi	Maa tokhe pyar kendo ahyan
Sioux	Techihhila
Slovak	Lu`bim ta
Slovenian	Ljubim te
Spanish	Te quiero / Te amo
Swahili	Ninapenda wewe
Swedish	Jag alskar dig
Swiss German	Ich lieb Di
Surinam	Mi lobi joe
Tagalog	Mahal kita

Taiwanese	Wa ga ei li
Tahitian	Ua Here Vau Ia Oe
Tamil	Nan unnai kathalikaraen
Telugu	Nenu ninnu premistunnanu
Thai	Chan rak khun (to male)
Thai	Phom rak khun (to female)
Turkish	Seni Seviyorum
Ukrainian	Ya tebe kahayu
Urdu	mai aap say pyaar karta hoo
Vietnamese	Anh ye^u em (to female)
Vietnamese	Em ye^u anh (to male)
Welsh	'Rwy'n dy garu di
Yiddish	Ikh hob dikh
Yoruba	Mo ni fe

Pheromones

“One kiss satisfies the hunger of two souls.”

–Sgt. Traci

What exactly are Pheromones?

Pheromones are chemicals that are secreted when we sweat. Although the Pheromones themselves don't have an odor or color, they have strong effects on behavior. Pheromones are believed to have a stronger influence on sexual attraction and drive than any other single factor!

How exactly do Pheromones work?

There is an organ in our nasal cavity called the Vomeronasal organ. This organ is the body's only receptor for pheromones. Other receptors in the nose do not respond to pheromones, but respond to normal scents like perfume and food aromas. The Vomeronasal organ does not respond to normal scents, but instead detects the odorless, barely perceptible pheromones. The Vomeronasal organ detects the Pheromones, and then causes biological reactions that affect our behavior (including sexual drive, desire, and choice of partners).

Pheromones from men are scientifically proven to increase the presence of the Luteinizing Hormone in women, which causes women to have a heightened sexual responsiveness toward the man secreting (or wearing) the Pheromones.

Pheromones from women are scientifically proven to increase Testosterone levels in men, which causes them to have a heightened sexual responsiveness to the woman secreting (or wearing) the Pheromones.

For your own love potion #9, try a squirt of this seduction in a bottle for $9.95-$49.95.

www.links2love.com (Click on "site index" on the top left side of the page.)

Planning Fun Things to Do

"Being in a happy relationship has nothing to do with your partner. You get back what you put into it."

–Sgt. Traci

Nation's Camping, RV Parks, and National Parks Guide

Your complete guide to the nation's most popular and hidden treasures.
www.nps.gov
www.gocampingamerica.com
www.camping.about.com/blaast.htm

River Rafting Trips and Tours

Your guide to water adventures..
www.landersrivertrips.com
www.raftingamerica.com
www.riversearch.com

Worldwide Hot Air Balloon Ride Directory

Your worldwide guide to fun in the sky
www.launch.net/rides.html

World Wide Bicycle Tour Directory

This is a comprehensive directory of for profit and non-profit bicycle tours and events. Bike touring companies or event directors input information directly into this database. These events and tours are a great way to learn about biking and will give you the opportunity to spend a beautiful day or vacation outdoors in the company of healthy and friendly bicyclists with nice legs. Have fun and bike your way to good health!

www.bicycletours.com

Scuba Diving Clubs and Trips Directory.

A real find to the nation's most popular and hidden treasures of the sea.
www.courseworld.com/links/diveclubs.html

Adventure Trips:

The Adventure Center offers walking and hiking vacations, cultural tours, African safaris, Antarctic expedition cruises, cultural tours, wildlife tours, family adventure vacations, cycling, mountain biking, rail journeys, overland expeditions, tall ship sailing, and much more with a range of over 700 adventure vacations worldwide. I have personal experience with this company; it is truly a gem!
www.adventurecenter.com

This is a small listing of outdoor adventure tour companies that will take you to do what you want to do, whether it be dog sledding, fishing, hunting, snowshoeing, trekking, safaris, or mountaineering...
www.adventuresports.com

Wild Horizons "Top 25 Adventure Trips" picks for world travel of 2005.
www.nationalgeographic.com/adventure/0411/excerpt1.html
www.nationalgeographic.com (click on Adventures and Explorations)

This website provides a worldwide index of limousine service companies with over 11,000 limo services. Find limos, sedans, stretch limousines, and SUVs for any occasion. Find one in your area today and enjoy.
www.limousineregistry.com

Golf Directory:

From the best maintained to the most challenging golf courses
www.truelocal.com
www.golfhelp.com

Family Fun:

Additional family fun suggestions (age appropriate) mini golf, bowling, go-karting, skee-ball competitions, Karaoke, paintball matches, board game challenges, and festivals.

Chuck E. Cheese where a kid can be a kid and an adult can act like one! Great for hosting Birthday parties; pizza, fun, and games; just type in your zip code to find the location nearest you.
www.chuckecheese.com/find

Dave and Busters is a facility that offers it all - food for the family, games for the kids, and bars for the adults. Find a location nearest you.
www.daveandbusters.com

The shrine circus is coming to town! Get your cotton candy, popcorn, and peanuts. Laugh at the clowns, watch the cannon catapult a human, and be mesmerized by the trapeze act. To find out when the circus will be visiting your city, type in your city or zip code for the events calendar, arrival dates, and admission prices
www.shrinecircus.com

This is a great directory that lists of all national Theme Parks, Amusement Parks, Water Parks, and Zoos, letting you search by state.
www.themeparkcity.com/USA_index.htm

Travel Resource Directory

"A sea of eyes and yet only two give flight to my heart."

–Sgt. Traci

Air/Land/Sea Quick Reference:

I have done the homework for you! Now you have no excuse to procrastinate before venturing on a romantic getaway! I have spent hundreds of hours writing, searching, researching, and putting together this book. After digging through the mounds and mounds of worthless trash on the internet, I have made the following website selections based on the sites that were the most user-friendly. Other selections were made based on positive personal experiences or credible recommendations. Believe me when I say that it was a very long and tedious process of elimination to weed out the clutter and the garbage and find the most valuable information! (These are not paid advertisements!)

Air:

A complete worldwide "Airline Directory" including toll free numbers and instant log on access to each individual website:
www.geocities.com/Thavery2000/

- American Airlines: www.aa.com or 1-800-433-7300
- Continental: www.continental.com or 1-800-433-7300
- Delta: www.delta.com or 1-800-221-1212
- Northwest: www.nwa.com or 1-800-225-2525
- Southwest Airlines: www.southwest.com or 1-800-I FLY SWA
- Ted Airlines: www.FlyTed.com
- TWA: 1-800-221-2000
- U.S. Air: www.usairways.com or 1-800-428-4322
- United: www.united.com or 1-800-241-6522
- www.airtreks.com or 1-877-AIRTREKS
- www.cheaptickets.com
- www.expedia.com
- www.priceline.com
- www.traveocity.com

Land:

Riding the Rails. Here is a complete directory of worldwide train service and schedules.
www.travelnotes.org or www.travelgate.co.uk

Take a bite out of the Big Apple. This service caters to all of your New York needs, wants, wishes, and desires:
www.nycvisit.com

Rent-A-Car Agencies:

- Alamo Rent-A-Car: (except FL)1-800-327-9633
- Avis Rent-A-Car: www.avis.com or 1-800-813-2847
- Budget Rent-A-Car: www.budget.com or 1-800-527-0700
- Canada/worldwide: 1-800-268-8900
- Dollar Rent-A-Car: www.dollar.com 1-800-421-9849
- Enterprise Rent-A-Car: www.enterprise.com
- Hertz Rent-A-Car: www.hertz.com 1-800-654-3131
- National Car Rental: www.nationalcar.com 1-800-328-4567
- Thrifty Rent-A-Car: www.thrifty.com 1-800-367-2277

Accommodations:

A worldwide directory of Bed and Breakfast facilities.
www.bedandbreakfast.com

A worldwide directory of hotels:
www.hotelsonline.com or www.inn26.com

A nation wide accommodation listing for pet lovers:
www.pets-allowed-hotels.com

To find a spa location nearest you, type in your zip code:
www.spafinder.com or www.spaindex.com

Sea:

A complete Cruise Line website directory categorizing your interests: River Cruises, themed cruises, alternative life style cruises, expedition cruises, economy cruises, luxury cruises, and ultra luxury cruises etc...
www.oceancruises.com
www.cruiseshopping.com/cruiselines.htm
www.vacationstogo.com

Top 100 Most Romantic Hotels of the World:

This is a nice collection of the 100 most romantic hotel accommodations. However, they neglected to include my personal favorite, "The Grand Wailea Resort Hotel and Spa Grande" on Maui, Hawaii:
www.grandwailea.com
www.romanticplaces.com

To find the top picks of just about everything, including Forbes pick of the World's Most Romantic Hotels 2005:
http://www.forbes.com/lifestyle/2005/02/10/cx_vg_0210feat_ls.html

Top 50 Most Romantic Dining Places in the United States:

This features a collection of romantic dining facilities in America.
http://honeymoons.about.com/od/specialoccasions/a/RomanticDining.htm

For other useful information:
www.honeymoons.about.com

Top 50 Most Romantic Getaway Places in the World:

Featuring a list of the top 50 most romantic places in the world, results from Modern Bride's Magazine Travel Agent Poll.
http://honeymoons.about.com/cs/10topspots/a/top50spots2003.htm

Packing Check List

- Airline Tickets/E-tickets
- Passport/ Birth Certificate/ Visa/ Marriage License
- Cash/ ATM Card/ Travelers' Checks/ Credit Card
- Photo Copies of Travelers' Checks & Important Documents
- Hotel Confirmation/ Emergency Contact Info./ Traveler Insurance
- Beach/Pool Wear
- Photo ID or Drivers License
- Camera/Camcorder/Film/Battery Backup
- Rental Car/Limo/Ride Arrangements
- Romantic Travel Bag (Music, Candles, Massage Oils etc.)
- Child Care Arrangements
- Sleep Wear/Lingerie
- Day Wear
- Snack Food for the Plane
- Dummy Wallet
- Sunscreen/Shades/Cap
- Toiletries
- Evening Wear/ Accessories
- Formal Wear
- Hair Dryer and Travel Iron
- Travel-Sized Games
- Kennel Arrangement for Pet
- Travel Umbrella
- Light or Heavy Jacket/Coat (Seasonal)
- Voltage Converter (International Travel)
- Medication
- Workout Wear

Weather:

Check the weather at your vacation destination.
National Weather Service:
301-763-8155 – www.nws.noaa.gov

USA Today's Weather & Travel Hotline:
1-900-932-8437 – www.usatoday.com/ads.htm
www.weather.com

Passport Information:

This site will allow you to find the nearest location to apply for a passport. It is provided by the Department of State's Bureau of Consular Affairs, Office of Passport Services/Customer Service, which designates many post offices, clerks of court, public libraries, and other state, county, township, and municipal government offices to accept passport applications on its behalf.
http://iafdb.travel.state.gov/

Lost or Stolen Credit card or Travelers Check:

Call all of these numbers to report the theft or loss of credit card:

- Equifax: 1-888-766-0008
- Experian: (formerly TRW) 1-888-397-3742
- Trans Union: 1-800-888-4213
- Social Security Administration: also has a fraud line if you think you've been a victim of identity theft. 1-800-269-0271

Lastly, Call Your Credit Card Company:

- American Express: 1-800-528-4800 (except AZ)
- Diners Club: 1-800-234-6377 (except CO)
- Mastercard: 1-800-826-2181
- Visa: 1-800-227-6800 for CA 1-800-632-4730
- Discover card: 1-800-DISCOVER

Get Cash Fast:

- Money Grams: 1-800-926-9400
- Western Union: 1-800-325-6000 – www.westernunion.com
- Credit Card Locators: 1-800-248-4286

Financial Planning

“The greatest treasure in all the world is found hidden within the chest of our own heart…Love.”

–Sgt. Traci

In my worldly survey, two of the leading contributions to failed or troublesome relationships were caused by issues related to sex and money. In regard to the first issue, it is no secret that men complain that they don't get enough sex and woman complain that they don't get their emotional needs met ... and since this seems to be common knowledge, why then does it seem so difficult for men to figure out that they are likely to receive more sex when they "romance" their partner more? I hope that this statement of the obvious will help some of you! Although romance does not require money, a lack of money can affect your levels of romance and place a strain on your relationship. It is important to have your financial house in order if you want to be a healthy, happy couple. A lack of resources adds pressure and strain to day to day living and puts one more obstacle between you and romantic time with your partner. You can alleviate financial issues and develop strategic financial plans for day to day living and for retirement (401K & IRA's) by choosing and using a good financial planner. I have personal experience with Family Financial, LLC near Milwaukee, Wisconsin, and as a result, have completely re-defined my financial future. I highly recommend that you work with one of their staff and begin creating a blue print for getting to where you want to be financially. Visit www.familyfin.com for a location they recommend nearest you. Another option to help get your finances in order is to get on Oprah's "Debt Diet" by logging onto www.oprah.com.

To begin making any changes in your life, financial or otherwise, start simple. Don't overload yourself. Set a goal and take at least one action towards achieving that goal each day. I began advidly (or as some say, obsessivly) setting goals in 2003, and I have kept a folder containing every single sheet since that time. Practice makes perfect, and it has been said that it takes at least 90 days of repetition for a new habit to set in and "stick." In my case, these statistics definitely ring true. I was a sloppy "goalie" for many months. And now, almost thoughtlessly and effortlessly, I average around 90% completion of my weekly goals. If I miss a goal one week, I roll it over to the next week and then I pay myself a penalty of $100 to an untouchable account or sometimes to charity for each goal that I missed. It is nice to thumb through my "goal" record book every once in a while to gauge a measurement of my progress and growth and view the direction of my changes and challenges.

I believe that anyone can accomplish, be, and achieve anything they choose if they possess these four attributes: vision, desire, belief, and follow through. Follow through requires great sacrifice and discipline. You have to look, choose, and move. There is no such thing as "try," you either do it or you don't! I hope you do!

"Everything in life comes down to two things:
dreaming it or doing it." –Sgt. Traci

Date: Accomplished ?	Yes/ No
SPIRITUAL GOALS:	
1.	
2.	
3.	
4.	
5.	
RELATIONSHIP GOALS:	
1.	
2.	
3.	
4.	
5.	
PERSONAL GOALS:	
1.	
2.	
3.	
4.	
5.	
CAREER GOALS:	
1.	
2.	
3.	
4.	
5.	
FINANCIAL GOALS:	
1.	
2.	
3.	
4.	
5.	
Projected Success Percent: Actual:	

Romance Rewards

“If science could harness only a fraction of the energy produced when two hearts collide, the lights of the world would burn all night.”

–Sgt. Traci

Cut out these Romance Rewards and use them as your ticket to paradise. Give them to your sweetie as a special treat, a reward, or for no reason at all. Slip one in a book he or she is reading, have one ready for him/her to discover in the cereal cabinet, place one on the seat or windshield of the car, or mail one to him or her at work so he or she has something to look forward to later. An added touch would be to copy or print the coupons on decorative or keepsake paper. Simply cut out desired coupons, staple together and present coupon booklet to your partner as a gift. Or, be creative and create your own custom "Romance Reward Coupons" for your sweetie.

Romance Rewards

For the One I Love

This "Romance Reward" Entitles You to One:

30 Minute Massage of Your Choice

For the One I Love

This "Romance Reward" Entitles You to One:

Night Of

____

For the One I Love

This "Romance Reward" Entitles You to One:

Night Of

____

For the One I Love

This "Romance Reward" Entitles You to One:

Your Night, Your Way

For the One I Love

This "Romance Reward" Entitles You to One:

Your Night, Your Way

For the One I Love

This "Romance Reward" Entitles You to One:

Breakfast in Bed
Dishes are on me

For the One I Love

This "Romance Reward" Entitles You to One:

Morning of Sleeping In

For the One I Love

This "Romance Reward" Entitles You to One:

$__________Shopping Spree

For the One I Love

This "Romance Reward" Entitles You to One:

***After Work, "Just Let Me Be" &
Give Me the Remote to Our TV***

For the One I Love

This "Romance Reward" Entitles You to One:

Full Detail Car Wash

For the One I Love

This "Romance Reward" Entitles You to One:

***Dog House, No Vacancy!
Get Out Of Jail Free!***

For the One I Love

This "Romance Reward" Entitles You to One:

Night Beneath the Stars

For the One I Love

This "Romance Reward" Entitles You to One:

Night of Snuggling
Nothing More...Nothing Less

For the One I Love

This "Romance Reward" Entitles You to One:

Lazy Day
Your Day, Your Way

For the One I Love

This "Romance Reward" Entitles You to One:

"YES" if I said "NO"
This Coupon Will Make Me Go

For the One I Love

This "Romance Reward" Entitles You to One:

Activity of Your Choice

For the One I Love

This "Romance Reward" Entitles You to One:

Benefit of the Doubt
No Questions Asked

For the One I Love

This "Romance Reward" Entitles You to One:

Sensuous Foot Bath or Rub

For the One I Love

This "Romance Reward" Entitles You to One:

Relaxing Bubble Bath

For the One I Love

This "Romance Reward" Entitles You to One:

Weekend of You & Me
No Phone, Kids, Distractions, or TV

For the One I Love

This "Romance Reward" Entitles You to One:

House Cleaning

For the One I Love

This "Romance Reward" Entitles You to One:

Deep Soul-Stirring Passionate French Kiss

For the One I Love

This "Romance Reward" Entitles You to One:

Romantic Picnic

For the One I Love

This "Romance Reward" Entitles You to One:

Romantic Walk Along the Beach

For the One I Love

This "Romance Reward" Entitles You to One:

____

For the One I Love

This "Romance Reward" Entitles You to One:

____

For the One I Love

This "Romance Reward" Entitles You to One:

____

For the One I Love

This "Romance Reward" Entitles You to One:

____

For the One I Love

This "Romance Reward" Entitles You to One:

____

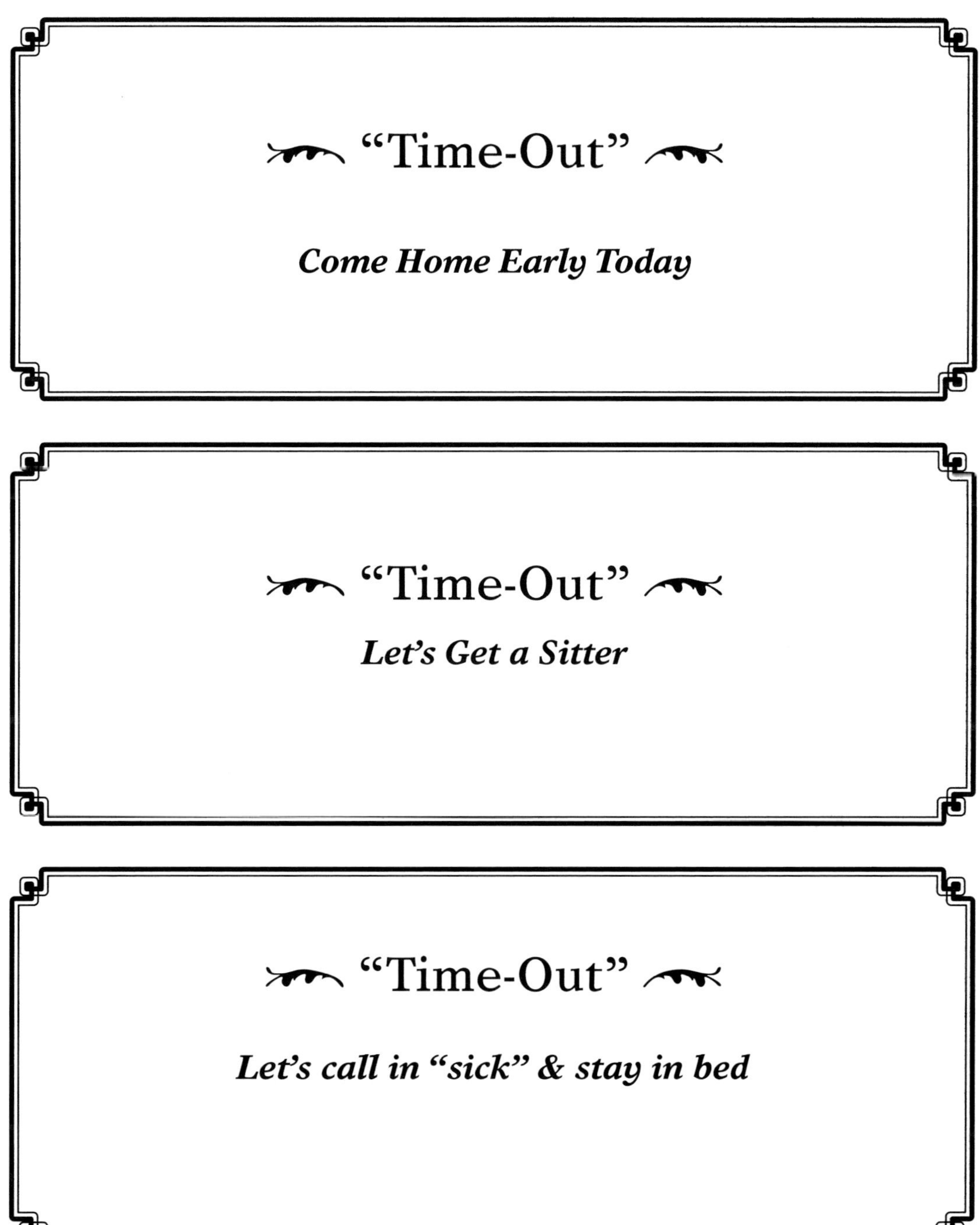
"Time-Out"
Come Home Early Today
"Time-Out"
Let's Get a Sitter
"Time-Out"
Let's call in "sick" & stay in bed

"Time-Out"

Let's get a sitter to take the children out while we stay in

"Time-Out"

I'm feeling a little neglected lately. What I need most is a little TLC from you.

"Time-Out"

I feel like we haven't been communicating lately. I'd really appreciate a heart to heart talk

"Time-Out"

Have I told you lately,
how much I appreciate you?
I just want you to know that
just because I don't say it often ...
Doesn't mean that I don't feel it often!

"Time-Out"

I'm Sorry. Can we talk?

"Time-Out"

I'm feeling a little insecure lately.
It would mean a lot to have some
reassurance from you.

I hope that this book has inspired you to plan many romantic dates for your sweetheart. I also hope that this book has reminded you that romance doesn't have to be elaborate or planned. The simple, daily things count too ... often much more than the occasional big dates. After a long day at work there is nothing nicer that being greeted with a warm hug or a tender kiss. Many times we take for granted the erotic, sensual, and loving act of hugging and kissing. Asking someone about his/her day and really listening for an answer is a huge step toward increasing intimacy in a relationship. Try loosening or removing your partner's tie or slipping off his/her shoes while they tell you about the day. Walk out to the car and help with bags, packages, or groceries without being asked. The simple act of greeting a spouse or significant other with a favorite beverage and the offer of a five minute foot rub could be a perfect ending to any challenging day. The offer alone truly speaks volumes to your sweetheart, letting him/her know that you care and are thinking about him/her, whether you are taken up on the invitation or not.

Romance is all about thought, imagination, and personalization. I hope you enjoyed the ideas presented here and I sincerely hope that romance abounds in your life daily!

Useless Tidbits about this Book, from the Author:

The note card Invitation "For the One I Love" concept began as a personal love-letter for a very special someone. It is a one of a kind twenty-three-page bound booklet of "choice" driven romantic interludes, which were never to be redeemed.

This book that you are holding was never intended to become a published "book" for the public. It was written with the initial intent to be given as a personal and sentimental gift to selected friends and family.

While the actual text flowed out of me almost thoughtlessly and effortlessly, the journey to compose this book from conception to delivery still took nearly three years. It took longer to prepare it for publishing than it did to write it!

These pages were typed using my own two fingers, all 61,000 words. Yours truly is now considering a keyboarding class when time permits.

Because I really didn't know I was writing a "book" when I began typing, this entire book was written using a program I had little knowledge about, a painful mistake I will never make again! In hindsight, I could have written another book instead of all the aggravation and wasted man hours I experienced.

My two grandmothers were the only two people allowed to read the manuscript and offer input during the writing phase.

For nearly a four month period, I obsessively sat in front of the computer screen for no less than 16 hours per day...seven days a week! There were times when I took less than 50 steps in a day! The first final draft was completed on my birthday, March 5th, 2005; my family literally had to peel me away from the computer to celebrate my birthday.

Backpacking around the world and conquering my terror of leaping from the world's highest Bungee jump - combined - proved easier than getting a book published!

The original name of this book was "Sensual Baths & Evenings" it was renamed several times, including Romance-911, before becoming

Romance-411: A Tactical Guide for the Romantically Challenged, just a month before my publishing deadline.

The book cover also went through several permutations, changing for the final time just weeks before publishing, due to unsuccessful attempts and growing costs of having my original (and favorite) cover idea designed.

This manuscript was rejected by nearly 100 publishing houses and agents before finally becoming a published book. Where there is a will there is a way!

"Us" Begins With "U"

2-Day Intensive

"The secret to having a happy and healthy 'US' is to have a happy and healthy 'U'!" -Sgt. Traci

- **Are you ready to learn the truth about yourself and the power of "U"?**
- **Are you ready to see your dreams and goals within reach and learn the skills you need to grab them?**
- **Are you ready to take all your relationships to a new level of understanding and honesty?**
- **Are you ready to live your life from choice, design, and purpose rather than reaction, obligation, and circumstance?**
- **Are you ready to experience one of the hardest and one of the most rewarding 48 hours of your inner personal life?**

If you are ready to raise the bar in your life, sign up for Sgt. Traci's Boot Camp! It completes the pyramid of knowledge which is Interest, Information, and Experience. While it is true that Romance-411 and the Operation Romance Web site are great sources of information and interest; if you only use these recourses, but never experience what the Boot Camp offers, you will only have two sides of your pyramid.

Relationships are things we experience on more than just an intellectual level. "They don't teach lion training through a correspondence course," Sgt. Traci says. That's why Sgt. Traci developed her experiential Boot Camp. It is at this Boot Camp that most people (Recruits) have their moments of insight and recognition. Sgt. Traci's Boot Camp is emotionally charged, but change is emotional and relationships are emotional, that's why many people have found that the benefits they received from attending the Boot Camp have changed their lives.

You know that "Us" Begins With "U" now you need to feel it too!

More money from your job, more sex in your marriage, more productivity from your employees, or more A's on your transcript; these are all the byproducts of the relationships you have with others. Having any or all of these things is merely a matter of learning the skills to improve the relationship at the center of all these; the relationship with "U." Sgt. Traci teaches you how.

By enlisting in Sgt. Traci's powerful Boot Camp you will learn:

- **How to be vulnerable. Vulnerability is one of the greatest skills that will help you strengthen and enrich your relationships.**

- **How to let go of the past issues affecting and infecting your current relationship.**

- **How to develop the Art of Listening and Communicating.**

- **How to target obstacles that stand between you and the life you desire.**

- **How to be more conscious of your self-talk and to identify your language of limitation.**

- **How to replace your bad habits with good habits.**

- **To commandeer abundance into your life.**

- **The skills to balance family, career, pleasure, and finances.**

- **To be accountable! Your word is your bond beginning today!**

- **To design your daily "Power Hour."**

- **To create a 90 day contract of habit and contract of honor.**

- **The five step process for turning dreams into reality.**
- **How to set a block of personal, relationship, career, spiritual/ tithing, and financial goals and develop a working mission statement to support them.**
- **To build a support team, action plan, and deadline to achieve your goals.**

One thing is for certain; if you don't act today it is unrealistic to assume that tomorrow will be any different then yesterday.
LOOK! CHOOSE! MOVE!

Enlist online now at www.OperationRomance.com and receive $50.00 off the regular Boot Camp enlistment price. Or, to register by phone, call: 1-877-4-SGT-TRACI and say "Draft Me Now"!

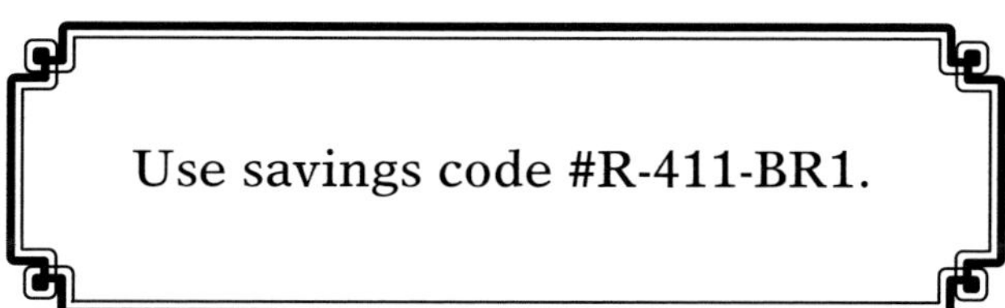

NOTES